Greg Dawson
and the
Psychology Class

by Jay E. Adams

TIMELESS TEXTS
Stanley, North Carolina

Foreword

By Jay E. Adams

I am happy to write this foreword at the request of Greg Dawson. All who are familiar with his valuable publication, *The Case of the "Hopeless Marriage,"*[1] know that Dawson is an accomplished nouthetic counselor. His first work was greeted by many as the finest available example of what nouthetic counseling is like, and people have been asking for more. Pastor Dawson, however, is for the near future "covered over" (as he puts it) with work at his church, especially because of the need to build an addition to provide more rooms for counseling. Evidently, people have been flocking to his First Scriptural Presbyterian Church[2] for help. He hopes at some time to publish another case study, but cannot say when that will be. He has consented, however, to let us in on some interviews about biblical counseling that recently took place. The interviews are of interest since the questions come from some young people taking a psychology course at a Christian university.

There are many who claim to do biblical – even nouthetic – counseling, but who don't have even the slightest idea about what it looks like. Some who do, sad to say, are sloppy about how they go about it, and others have brought in novel twists that distort the concepts inherent in true *nouthesia*. Dawson's answers to the students provide a needed correction. If you are told that someone is counseling nouthetically, but what he does doesn't match what you read in this book, you may have good reason to be suspicious.

I am happy that brother Dawson has consented to let us in on this series of interviews, since that gives him the opportunity to "set the record straight" about many matters as well as to set forth a number of things for which there was not room in his previous book. I hope that Greg will continue to

---

1. Stanley, NC: Timeless Texts, 2006.
2. A fictional church, so as to confuse no one.

write about counseling – a subject concerning which he shows much learning, wisdom and adroitness. Here's wishing – and praying – that this volume will meet as enthusiastic a success as his previous one did. I think you will find it eminently helpful.

Introduction

Ever since I allowed Jay Adams to talk me into publishing a case that he considers to be truly typical of nouthetic counseling I have been inundated by people wanting help. I have found it necessary not only to train my elders, but even my deacons to assist me.[1] Many Christians have not been adequately taught and cared for. Genuine biblical shepherding is difficult to find in the church. Because of this additional burden, I have only consented to give this account of some interviews with students at Christian University in order to satisfy those who want to learn more. They too have been asking for help. Instead of trying to answer all of my e-mails, along with my first book, I can now simply hand them a copy of this work.

If the language and the tone of my answers seem too familiar, jocular, or even caustic at times, I beg no special pardon for it. I have answered just the way I think each question should be answered, and make no apologies for it.[2] Straightforward talk in Christian circles is rare. I suppose one reason why I was drawn to nouthetic counseling is its *avowedly* biblical and exegetical approach. And, of nearly equal impor-

---

1. For those who need such training, I recommend the DVD distance learning program that is available from The Institute for Nouthetic Counseling (www.Nouthetic.org). This program is over 200 hours in length and covers just about every aspect of Christian counseling. Send for a free catalog.
2. I'm not denying that I frequently might have spoken more precisely had I not been answering off the cuff. But I wanted the material to be highly readable and to have an authentic character about it. I try – however successfully, I'm not sure – to be speaking to Phil and the others as though they were *you* interviewing *me*.

tance, you'll find that the inspired writers didn't pull punches. They frankly covered difficult subjects – predestination and election, divorce and remarriage, human responsibility and church discipline, wrath and damnation – and untiringly combated error, without batting an eye. Of course, I'm not an inspired apostle, but I have attempted to adopt the frank apostolic tone and attitude in my answers. Good students expect that. This book of answers arose spontaneously as replies to interviews from students studying psychology at a Christian college. Perhaps that fact will make the book more interesting. But, one way or another I hope it's something that God will approve. And, in the final place, that's what really counts.

CHAPTER ONE

Phil: Well, we've finally gotten together.

Greg Dawson: I'm glad we did, after jockeying around those dates.

Phil: Yes, and Pastor Dawson, I'm glad you were able to see me when you did. With the building I see going on outside, I suspect that you must be rather busy!

Greg: Well, enlarging a church building isn't the easiest thing, but we're thankful that we have to, in spite of the problems that it brings. God has greatly blessed us! By the way, call me "Greg."

Phil: OK. I'll remember that – Greg. And you can call me "Phil."

Greg: Good! Now, Phil, will you please fill me in a little more about why you wanted this interview?

Phil: Gladly. I'm working on my Ph.D. at Christian U,[1] and I was assigned the task of studying nouthetic counseling by our psychology professor. By the way, did I pronounce that correctly?

Greg: Unless you are a Greek student I wouldn't expect you to pronounce it properly. It's "nOOthetic" not "nAUthetic." It comes from the New Testament Greek word that refers to the biblical way of counseling.

Phil: Well, thanks. When I get back to class, I'll know how to say it! Can you tell me how this term came to describe your type of counseling and who came up with it?

Greg: Certainly. The word first appeared in the book *Competent to Counsel*, published in 1970 by Jay Adams, who coined the word as an English term to describe biblical counseling.

---

1. A fictitious name.

Phil: How did he come to choose this term?

Greg: Adams wanted a word that at once would accurately describe what biblical counseling is all about while, at the same time, would be unencumbered by previous ideas associated with other types of counseling. The words "Christian Counseling" and "Biblical Counseling" have become so broadly used today that they would not do. Good terms they are in themselves – you understand – but overworked so as to describe almost anything that a Christian might do when counseling, regardless of the content of his system. Under one of those labels he might even offer secular counseling thinly overlaid by a few Bible verses, or he might provide some sort of approach that misuses the Bible, as (for example) one such counselor did when he likened the Scriptures to a Rorschach test from which one extracts only what he previously projected into it!

Phil: Wow! I didn't know that people said things like that about the Bible.

Greg: They do. Indeed, this was a man who taught counseling at a large theological seminary! But you wanted to know more about nouthetic counseling...

Phil: Right. But before you go on describing it, can you tell me anything about this Adams person who coined the term?

Greg: OK. Adams is a conservative Presbyterian minister associated with the ARP denomination.[1] He has pastored several congregations, taught in two seminaries, and studied in three. He majored in Greek at Johns Hopkins University and received his Ph.D. from the University of Missouri in Speech. He was called to teach preaching in the department of Practical Theology at Westminster Theological Seminary in Philadelphia. As the "new man on the block" he also was assigned to teach a pastoral course with a segment pertaining to coun-

---

1. ARP stands for Associate Reformed Presbyterian church, which had its origins in Scotland.

seling that no one else wanted to teach. He had one year to prepare. Since in his own training he had little to go on, he immediately hit the books, reading everything on counseling he could get his hands on. He even took a two-semester course at Temple University under a practicing Freudian psychologist – to no avail. None of it was compatible with his understanding of the Bible – and, to boot, it didn't work! So he began digging into the Bible with new fervor to discover what God had to say about helping people in trouble. Providentially, at that very time, O. Hobart Mowrer, a past president of the American Psychological Association, was speaking near the seminary, and Adams went to hear him. In a discussion following Mowrer's lecture he was invited to participate in a post-doctoral fellowship at the University of Illinois where Mowrer was a research professor. He accepted, and during his residence there he had the opportunity to work with Mowrer at two mental institutions and spend time in roundtable discussions with him and five other students. He came home firmly convinced that the non-Christian psychological ideas that he was still clinging to when he left for Illinois had to be abandoned, and that he must find answers in the Bible and nowhere else. "Mowrer," he said, "freed me to search the Scriptures alone, with no guilt at leaving psychology behind. For that, I will always be grateful. But I couldn't adopt his system, which conflicted with the Scriptures."[1] He then concentrated on Scripture alone and subsequently, while studying it and counseling ten hours a day, two days a week, came to the nouthetic position.

Phil: Well, you certainly seem to know a good bit about Adams and his work.

Greg: I should, Phil. I studied with him.

---

1. While appreciating the anti-psychological emphasis of this APA president, Adams flatly rejected Mowrer's Integrity Therapy system as completely unbiblical.

Phil: Can you tell me more about the word noothetic? What does it mean?

Greg: Sure. The Greek word is used by the apostle Paul to refer to the counseling he did (see Acts 20:20, 31; Colossians 1:28, for instance) and that which he encouraged others to do (see Romans 15:14; Colossians 3:16; I Thessalonians 5:12–14[1]). It has three components: loving verbal Confrontation out of Concern in order to bring about Change pleasing to God. Those three Cs say it all.

Phil: Good, that might provide me an interesting way to organize and present my paper to the graduate class in psychology. But I doubt that the history of the movement will sit well with the prof and some of the students!

Greg: Well, if so, that won't be the first time, I assure you. We're not out to make enemies, but we don't hesitate to set forth our differences and, sometimes, that stirs people up.

Phil: I can imagine. What I hear you saying, I think, is that psychology has no place in Christian counseling. Right?

Greg: You got it in one (as the Brits say)! But let me make one distinction. We see no place for *counseling* psychology. Some other departments of psychology are legitimate – study of how light falls on the retina and is ultimately perceived as color, for instance.

Phil: So you're also saying, if I don't mistake you, that the courses in psychology that I'm taking ought not to be taught at Christian U, and that I probably shouldn't be majoring in psychology. Correct?

Greg: You said it – well!

Phil: Then, what ought I to be studying if I want to help people?

---

1. In all of these passages the words *nouthesia* (n) and *noutheteo* (v) appear.

Greg: Courses leading to the ministry. That's the venue in which Christians ought to prepare themselves for a formal ministry of counseling. You don't need the courses you're taking to help people – what you need is proficiency in solid theology and exegesis of the biblical languages. Every counseling problem is a theological problem; every counseling solution is a theological solution. In other words, you should head for the ministry and go to seminary! There – you asked, and I said it!

Phil: Wow! You certainly did! But I guess I pushed you to do so didn't I?

Greg: Yes, but the discussion would probably have come round to that anyway. Phil, let me tell you about an experience Adams once had. He told us that he was invited to Georgia State University to speak to a graduate class taught by a Christian professor who thought that he could best prepare students for counseling by an eclectic mix of psychology and Bible (a theory usually called "integration"). Before accepting, Adams thought it right to inform the professor that he would have to speak on the topic "Why this Program Shouldn't Exist" – so that, if he cared to, he could withdraw the invitation. He was invited anyway, and lectured on the topic as stated. The next year he was again invited. He told the professor that he would repeat the message from the previous year, because it was still appropriate. Curiously, he was invited again. And – you've got it – he said the same things to the next year's class! So, what you have discovered today isn't something new to us, though I'm sure it is to you.

Phil: I see! Well, this Adams fellow must have stirred up a great deal of controversy – right?

Greg: At one time – when nouthetic counseling was new – it seemed as though there'd be no end to it. Everywhere nouthetic counselors went they were attacked, and much false gossip was spread about them. But things have changed since the 70s and 80s. Other systems of counseling have come and gone and many people have become tired of retooling in order to adapt to the latest theory. Each new system has been debunked by the next until, today (except in those college and seminary campuses where little practice and much theorizing is done) the tone has changed radically. It used to be that when a nouthetic counselor spoke, many of the questions at the conclusion of his speech were hostile. But now, that has died down and the questions have largely become inquisitive. For example: "How do I do so-and-so? Tell me what to say in a thus-and-thus situation." A new breeze is blowing. Some of those in the institutions that still teach the old stuff ought to open their classroom windows!

Phil: Well, I suspect that I'm going to give quite a presentation to the class in two months! If nothing else, there ought to be a lot of interest! Actually, I've heard a number of students question some of the stuff we are being taught. And there's one very intelligent girl who brings in books to class and quotes from them in contradiction to what is being taught. I now wonder if they are nouthetic counseling books. Are there any in existence other than the one by Adams that you mentioned?

Greg: Very many. Adams, himself, has written over one hundred books – mostly on biblical counseling. Before you leave I'll give you a couple. I keep a supply on hand. Now that nouthetic counseling has become a movement, there are numerous other authors who have written books as well. As a matter of fact, one of my own counseling cases has been published by Timeless Texts under the title, *The Case of the "Hopeless Marriage."* I'll give you a copy of that one too.

Phil: Great!

Greg: Oh oh! I see the foreman on the building project heading this way. He may interrupt us for a bit if he has a question…Sure enough, that's him knocking at the door. Come in, Frank. Frank, this is Phil, who is interviewing me for a presentation to his University class. What can I do for you?

Frank: Happy to meet you, Phil. You'll learn a lot from Greg. I'm sorry to interrupt, but this is important, Greg. Otherwise I wouldn't disturb you. Can you come with me to look at something?

Greg: Well, if it's essential, Frank – of course.

Frank: I think it is.

Greg: OK, I'll be there in a minute. [Frank leaves.] I'll have to go for now, but it shouldn't be long, and if you can stay, I'll be back as soon as possible.

Phil: I'll wait.

Greg: Good. Here's something by Adams to read while you do. These are several short pamphlets he wrote on various subjects. You can find them in the waiting rooms of a number of Christian physicians, and in church tract racks. Perhaps you've seen them there. Enjoy them while I'm gone. See you as soon as possible.

Phil: Hope there's no serious problem. If there is, you may have to work your nouthetic counseling magic on it, or we'll have to continue at a later date!

CHAPTER TWO

[Pastor Greg enters the room to find Phil intently reading the last of the pamphlets – the one on depression.]

Phil: I'm amazed at how much has been compressed into these relatively short tracts.

Greg: Well, what did you think of them?

Phil: Let me say first, I'm happy for Frank's interruption because it gave me a chance to bone up on nouthetic counseling and to be able to ask more intelligent questions. I hope that the problem with the building wasn't too difficult...

Greg: No, just an important decision about some details. Shall we take up where we left off?

Phil: Frankly, I'd like to postpone some of those thoughts until we have time to discuss some things contained in these pamphlets.

Greg: That's fine with me Phil. Shoot!

Phil: One obvious factor is that in every pamphlet there is a Gospel message and an appeal to believe it. How is that? I believe in evangelism, but why would that be a part of one's counseling concerns?

Greg: Good question! Evangelism and edification (and counseling is a part of the latter) stand together – they cannot be separated except at great peril.

Phil: Why do you say that? I thought you could counsel without evangelizing.

Greg: Theoretically, that may be so, but practically, on the day-by-day level, it simply isn't possible. You can't truly counsel until effective evangelism has been carried out. Conversion is essential for biblical counseling to take place.

Phil: How is that?

Greg: We don't knowingly counsel unbelievers.

Phil: What? That's a new wrinkle.

Greg: An unbeliever can't do anything to please God. Romans 8:8 assures us that "those who are in the flesh [that is unbelievers] *cannot* please God." We are not called to the task of helping unbelievers move from one lifestyle that displeases God to another that equally displeases Him. And that's exactly what we'd be doing if we attempted to counsel unbelievers. Liberals do it all of the time; but we're not liberals! Sadly, some genuine Christians who counsel don't get the point either.

Phil: Does that mean you refuse to do good to unbelievers?

Greg: No, just the opposite. It does no good to make them think that a new lifestyle that displeases God is a better one, although they may find some relief through it. The point is that it does them no eternal good, and may do irreparable harm. We don't knowingly counsel unbelievers – we evangelize them. We know that they don't have the capacity to follow biblical directions in ways that will honor God, and so we make it clear that something else must come first.

Phil: You *tell* him you are going to evangelize him?

Greg: Well, not exactly; not in so many words. After having listened to some of his difficulties, we may say something like this: "These are serious problems, but God has answers to all of them. However, you're not in a position to avail yourself of those answers. So we must *precounsel* you." It's an accurate term that, for us, means "evangelize." And it makes it perfectly clear to the unbeliever we cannot yet begin to counsel him. Something else must come first. If you use the term "evangelize," he may think of people rolling down sawdust aisles in a tent flapping in the wind. So we precounsel him.

Phil: Then, how do you determine who is and who isn't a true believer?

Greg: Since God alone can look into someone's heart – sometime check out II Chronicles 6:30 [Phil makes a note in his notebook.], we must take his word and the word of the church to which he belongs that he is a Christian – provided that it is an evangelical congregation that cares for the sheep and practices church discipline. Until that matter is settled we do not counsel. Moreover, the Personal Data Inventory that we have everyone fill out has questions that are crafted so as to be able to make at least a rough assessment of the potential counselee's faith. We can never be absolutely certain, of course – because we aren't God – but we take every legitimate biblical caution about the matter. And, though we may sometimes misjudge, we are rarely wrong.

Phil: What happens if the evangelism fails – if the person refuses to believe?

Greg: I'm sure you understand from what I've said, that we go on evangelizing him as long as he will listen. If he is about to quit, we urge him to think carefully about the God he is abandoning, and we usually slip a Gospel burr into his saddle, so that as he rides off into the sunset, it will irritate him into thinking more about the matter. I understand that Adams often uses Proverbs 13:15, "The way of transgressors is hard," as a burr, and assures such a person that he is always willing to help when he finds this to be true and returns. Some do remember the verse and do return – not all, of course.

Phil: So, was Gary Collins right or wrong when he said that Adams doesn't believe in doing good for unbelievers?

Greg: Wrong! Quite wrong. Gary hasn't read it carefully. What Adams is saying is that we don't ask unbelievers to do the good that God requires – because they can't. For them to try would make them hypocrites, and perhaps even give them a dangerous, false assurance that mere outward actions please God. God wants hearts as well as behavior, and the heart commitment must come first! Otherwise, a person may become a

Pharisee. There are already too many Pharisees – we don't have to help people become Pharisees!

We most assuredly do believe in helping unbelievers by aiding them with food, shelter, clothing, money, and so on. Collins' misunderstanding may have come from the gossip about nouthetic counseling that travels around. Please scotch it whenever you hear it next. Speaking of gossip, many think that nouthetic counselors believe every problem is the result of one's sin. Many problems are, but not all trouble results from a counselee's personal disobedience to God; trouble can result from another person sinning against him, causing him serious difficulties. Naturally, we live in a world where there is much trouble on every hand – all of which, ultimately, is the result of sin: i.e., the sin of Adam and Eve in the Garden of Eden. But that isn't the same as consequences from personal sin committed after the fall. The two should not be confused. In *Competent to Counsel,* published in 1970, Adams thought that he had guarded against any such accusation by citing the examples of Job and the man mentioned in John 9 who was born blind. Both cases demonstrate the fact that trouble may not result from one's own personal sin. He mentioned these cases to disabuse any one from misunderstanding this matter since he *did* have to say much about the place of sin in counseling. Yet, today – a full generation after the book was written – people still accuse us of saying that all of one's problems stem from one's own personal sin. This is what I mean by gossip – ideas thrown about by those who have never carefully studied our writings.

Phil: I'm surprised to hear this, since I was told that very rumor. I think the class will be surprised too. Perhaps even our prof – if he has accepted gossip!

Greg: Go easy on him, Phil. After all, if he hasn't read nouthetic counseling materials carefully, he may be using his graduate students to fill him in. Perhaps your report will intrigue him enough to urge him to study further. I suggest that you make the oral report short and to the point, and be ready to field questions. Give him the full picture in the written report, but leave the details and side issues for the Question-and-Answer section.

Phil: It's been a long day and this interview has been so illuminating that I need time to think about it. Could I return next week to continue? I do want to discuss those matters in the pamphlets you handed me.

Greg: Certainly. I'll count on it, and set time for it in my schedule. And, in the meantime, here are a couple of books. [He hands him *Competent to Counsel* and *The Case of the "Hopeless" Marriage*.] Now, let's pray about our discussion. [Greg prays.][1]

---

1. I make a point of never simulating prayer.

CHAPTER THREE

[It has been one week since the last interview took place. According to schedule, Phil shows up at Greg's office. He is accompanied by a girl.]

Phil: Good to see you again, Pastor Greg. This is Jane, the classmate I told you about who brings books to class and debates the psychology professor. I hope you don't mind her tagging along.

Greg: The more the merrier! Hello Jane, I'm happy to meet you.

Jane: Thank you for letting me come. I'm very much interested in what Phil told me concerning your last interview. I...

Phil: [breaking in] And I thought you'd be interested to know that it *is* Adams' books that she brings to class! Sorry to interrupt, Jane.

Jane: That's all right. I was just going to say something like that myself.

Phil: I guess I was so anxious to tell Pastor Greg that I forgot my manners!

Greg: Well, having both of you here is a bonus, so far as I'm concerned. I'm delighted you could come Jane.

Jane: Thank you.

Greg: Where would you like to begin, Phil?

Phil: Well, Jane and I have been talking things over a lot during the week, and I suspect she knows about all I learned from my last visit. In fact, she told me some more things that we didn't have time to get around to. And she's going to help me with my report – it's due next month, you know. So that will be a big boost. Right! I wasn't too sure when I took on this assignment that I'd find much that was interesting, but between you and Jane I've become fascinated with nouthetic counseling and want to learn everything I can about it.

Jane: I told Phil about some of the other aspects of the move-ment – including the formation of counseling training cen-ters, of training through a distance learning program on DVD and the existence of an accrediting body. These were all new things to Phil, and he seemed impressed that nouthetic coun-seling isn't merely the small, esoteric organization that he had imagined.

Greg: Good! And we'll do all we can to help you – right, Jane?

Jane: Exactly, I think from what I've seen of Phil, he'd make a great pastor if he adopted a nouthetic stance toward the min-istry.

Phil: Well, that's sorta' what you told me last week, Greg. I hope you two won't gang up on me. I've thought about the ministry, but I'm not ready to commit myself to it by any means.

Greg: Give him time and space, Jane. If God wants him, he'll go; he'll head in that direction soon enough. If he goes on his own, he ought not! Now, where should we begin this week?

Phil: I thought I'd like to discuss the pamphlet on depression a bit. Now, I've read it several times, and I know what Adams has to say. But…

Greg: Can you articulate the fundamental issue involved?

Phil: Sure. According to the pamphlet, in a true depression (not a merely "blue" day) a person has ceased to fulfil his reg-ular activities – housework, grading papers, etc. Things have been piling up. As the piles get larger the depressed person feels even worse because he knows they are there and not being dealt with. But since he feels worse, he has further rea-son to neglect them, and so the pile continues to grow. Even-tually, he may go to bed and try to forget the whole thing, but responsibilities go on piling up just the same. Others may consider him sick – or mentally ill – when actually, he is only being irresponsible. Have I got it right?

Greg: Not bad. You've laid your finger on the fundamental problem. But how does a person get himself – or herself – into such a fix in the first place?

Jane: I know the answer to that. Something gets the person down – he doesn't feel like assuming responsibilities. So, he lets them slide. The one critical element that Phil missed in his description of the downward spiral is the fact that the person fails to do various chores because he is following his feelings rather than carrying out his responsibilities.

Greg: Good! That's a key point. Of course, it isn't "something" that gets him down; he gets himself down over something or other. Now, can either of you tell me how a counselor would advise him?

Phil: I think that he'd tell him to buck up, things aren't that bad, and that he ought to get back to work.

Jane: No! No! He'd never tell him to buck up or that things aren't all that bad. Indeed, he'd agree with him that things may be bad, difficult or tough, but he'd also explain that he has made them even worse by following his feelings instead of carrying out his responsibilities. That part you got right, Phil.

Greg: With Jane here, I can see that I don't need to do all of the talking.

Jane: I didn't mean to take over.

Greg: Oh, that's not a problem. I'm just so glad to listen to someone who knows what she's talking about. You're right, Jane, we never minimize true difficulties but, at the same time, we maximize the power of God to enable us to meet them. Indeed...

15

Jane: I know, you're about to quote I Corinthians 10:13, where Paul said that God never sends anything into a believer's life that he can't handle, if he handles it God's way!

Greg: Yes. I might have eventually mentioned that verse, since it's such a hope-giving one. But I was about to say that one can emerge from a depression by repenting of his sin and failures. For example, a housewife who fails to prepare meals for the family because she doesn't feel like it, or a preacher who gives poor sermons because he has allowed himself to become discouraged and doesn't prepare his messages properly. After repenting of sin, one must then assume the neglected responsibilities – *no matter how he or she feels*. Again, that's the key.

Phil: Well, is that all that's necessary? Isn't depression some dark, mysterious state as we've been told?

Greg: It can be a very dark state, but there's nothing mysterious about it. God made us in such a way that when we do right, we feel right; when we do wrong, we feel wrong – sometimes very wrong indeed![1]

Phil: Well, how long does it take for a depressed person to emerge from his depression?

Jane: I know that it took my mother only two weeks. The first week she might have done so, but she kept allowing her feelings to get in the way. Once she repented and prayerfully plowed ahead as her nouthetic counselor told her – in spite of all of her feelings to the contrary – she quickly came out of her depression. As she saw the "pile" going down, her spirits began to rise.

Phil: Really? And all the time I thought that a cure was something that took months – or even years – to pull off!

Jane: It was through the help the nouthetic counselor gave my mother that I became interested in it. After all, my mother's

---

1. See Genesis 4:7 (NASB).

depression had been chronic. It was a terrible burden on my dad and the rest of the family. What a blessing when her life changed!

Phil: Has it ever returned?

Jane: Never.

Phil: How long ago did this happen?

Jane: Seven years ago.

Greg: Jane's mother's experience is typical. Now let me refer you to a biblical rationale for this. Phil, you seem to know something about the New Testament. Can you tell me what Paul's life as a missionary was like?

Phil: Pretty tough, I'd say. There are those two long passages in II Corinthians where he details what he endured.

Greg: Right. Wouldn't you say that if there was anyone who might get depressed, it would be Paul?

Phil: I guess that's right, but I never thought about it before.

Greg: *Did* he become depressed?

Phil: No way. He kept on preaching in spite of everything – beatings, stoning, imprisonment – you name it!

Greg: Exactly. But he was human. He had feelings too! Don't you think that he must have wanted to quit from time to time?

Jane: I know I'd want to.

Phil: I'm pretty sure I would too.

Greg: But he didn't. [Greg turns to his Bible.] Indeed, here's what he said: "As a result, we don't give up, even though our outer person is decaying, because our inner person is being renewed daily" (II Corinthians 4:16). In chapter four he says a lot about how he avoided depression (which, in essence is "giving up" on your responsibilities). For instance, in verses eight and nine he says, "We are afflicted in all sorts of ways, but not crushed; perplexed, but not given to despair; perse-cuted, but not deserted; struck down, but not destroyed." A depressed person is "crushed, given to despair." He has "given up." How did Paul, who certainly couldn't have *felt* like going on after the stoning at Lystra, overcome his feelings so as to continue? In verse one he tells us: "Therefore, since we have this service to perform as the result of mercy, we don't give up." Paul was so grateful for his salvation and his appoint-ment to the apostolic ministry that he would perform God's service or "ministry" until God told him to stop. That's the key. Motivated by gratitude for the good things, one can endure and overcome the bad ones. Paul went on *regardless* of how he felt. When a person is tempted to lay aside his respon-sibilities because he doesn't feel like doing them (for whatever reason), yet understands God's goodness to him and seeks to please Him by assuming those responsibilities anyway, he will not become depressed.

Phil: Makes sense to me. And, though it may be hard, you're right, it *isn't* a mystery.

Jane: And, don't forget I Corinthians 10:13. There Paul gives three reasons for going on rather than succumbing to the temptation to do otherwise. First, your problems are those "which other people have experienced." That is, they are not unique. Others have gone through them successfully. Second, "God is faithful Who will not allow you to be tried beyond what you are able to bear" – if, of course you do so His way. Third, there will be a way out. The testing will not go on for-ever. Those promises alone could keep one going on rather than giving up!

Greg: How right you are Jane!

Phil: I can see that too. There's a lot more to nouthetic coun-seling than I thought. And I especially like the fact that it is so clearly Bible-based. Why haven't I learned these things before? Here I am going to a Christian university and I'm not being taught what the Bible says about such things. That shouldn't be.

Greg: No, it shouldn't. And, perhaps, some day when you have become a minister of the Gospel or a Christian business-man, you will be able to do something about it. Right now, you can pray and make the truth known in your various spheres of influence.

Phil: At least Jane doesn't buy psychology even now. And she speaks up. I notice that when she does so, she's polite but firm, and seems to know what she's talking about; and I think others in the class are impressed. I hope my class report will convince some too.

Jane: I'll be praying that it will. I'm taking this course only because it's required; not because I wanted to. But, in fact, it's actually strengthened my belief in nouthetic counseling, since it has shown me very clearly that psychology doesn't have the answers.

Greg: I'll pray too. Phil, it sounds like you've almost been sold on nouthetic counseling. Am I right? Jane is already there.

Phil: Well, I think I might be getting there too. I will want to see what happens next month when I give the report – what the prof says, and how the class responds. If they can't refute it, then I may come round.

Greg: Don't base your beliefs and practices on what others say or think; be sure that what you believe and do grows out of and is consistent with the Scriptures at every point. That's the avowed purpose of nouthetic counselors.

Jane: It's lunch time! Let's go eat.

Greg: Good idea, and spoken nouthetically! I'd lost track of the time, but my stomach tells me you're right. I'll treat. And we'll postpone any more talk until after lunch, OK?

Phil & Jane: OK!

CHAPTER FOUR

[One hour and a half later all three return, having enjoyed their meal.]

Greg: I hope we'll be able to talk sensibly after such a lunch! You know, the worst two times to preach are just before a meal, when everyone wants to leave and eat, and just after, when they feel like dozing.

Jane: Well, I for one am ready. I think it's just great to see Phil becoming acquainted with nouthetic counseling.

Phil: I guess I am too. Thanks for the lunch; I've always enjoyed Chick-fil-A®.

Jane: And I understand that it was begun by a Christian!

Greg: OK. What now? After all, this is your interview; take it away Phil.

Phil: What are some of the "mechanics" (for lack of a better word) – I mean how does nouthetic counseling work? What happens in a counseling session?

Greg: You're wise to ask that question. People can say that they do biblical counseling, but when you examine what actually goes on in their counseling sessions, you may think otherwise. It's in the practice that a counselor's true presuppositions and beliefs most clearly emerge.

Jane: I never thought of it that way before. See, Phil, you're already beginning to ask good questions – just like a nouthetic counselor!

Greg: Well, I can't tell you everything in the short time that we have, but you can find out exactly what happens by precept, in Adams' *The Christian Counselor's Manual*, and by example, in my book, *The Case of the "Hopeless Marriage."* What we can do here is to try to answer any particular questions that you may have about our methodology.

Phil: Fair enough. Tell me, what place does prayer have in nouthetic counseling?

Greg: Prayer is important to us. We pray before sessions, use our counseling session notes as reminders to pray for particular items between sessions, and we pray at the conclusion of every session. There are times of special breakthroughs when we might thank God in the session, or when things are confused or difficult.

Jane: Yes, prayer is important. You know the saying, "Prayer changes things."

Greg: Jane, I'm surprised at you. You know as well as I that prayer doesn't change things; it's God who does. There are counselors who believe that the act of praying is "therapeutic" (to use their term) regardless of the "god" to whom you pray.

Jane: Whoops! I guess what I said wasn't very nouthetic after all. I know that nouthetic counselors warn against "old sayings" because many of them have no basis in Scripture and will, therefore, lead people astray. I remember someone saying that the old saying, "You can't teach an old dog new tricks," is wrong and convinces people who believe it that they are stuck in their present behavior patterns. Objection sustained!

Phil: Well, now wait a minute! You don't mean to say that nouthetic counselors are super conscious about language, do you?

Greg: That's exactly what I say. Language has meaning. Words are not merely "signs" as the linguists claim. They are also sign *posts*! For instance, when a politician sins, it seems that the practice now-a-days is to call that a "mistake." Naturally, every sin is a mistake; but it's far more than that. Basically, it's an offense against a holy God. To call it a mistake is, therefore, a mistake – and nothing more than a poor excuse! To call it "sin" is to point to Jesus Christ. After all, He came to deal with sin!

Jane: And, whenever someone calls a sin a "sickness," he points his counselee to a physician rather than to Jesus Christ, Who forgives sin. Physicians can't do that.

Greg: Right! Now, you've redeemed yourself, Jane. But, let me point out, we never call anything by the name "sin" unless the Scriptures say it is. We are not legalists who compose our own lists of sin. Moreover, we understand that calling homosexuality, for instance, something other than sin takes away the hope of leaving it behind. Calling something sin that really is sin brings hope precisely because Jesus came to deal with sin, as Jane indicated. To call it a sickness, or a genetic problem, when it really isn't, destroys hope. So, using the label "sin" properly is a kindness that nouthetic counselors show to their counselees.

Phil: And all the time I thought that it was cruel to tell a counselee that he's a sinner.

Greg: It never is when what you are talking about is clearly called a sin in the Scriptures. God's ways – and His words – are never cruel.

Jane: And what about this matter of labeling? Pastor, tell him what we think about that.

Greg: Since you brought it up, why don't you do so Jane?

Jane: Gladly. Labeling is important because people, even the one labeled, begins to think of himself in that way. Tell someone he's schizophrenic or has multiple personalities, and he'll begin to act like it's true. It's important to gum only those labels on people's files that you can find in Strong's concordance (I didn't make that up – I heard someone say it). So, what that means is that we should do away with psychological jargon and use biblical terms or descriptions alone.

Greg: Well said, Jane! You see, Phil, nouthetic counselors are acutely aware of the impact of language and want to be extremely careful about what they say. The problem is that some who think that they are nouthetic – or are trying to be –

are sloppy in their use of terminology. And, as a result, they confuse themselves. Some – I don't know why, perhaps it's to sound "scientific" or "academic" – even use psychological language. That's far from being nouthetic.

Phil: It seems as though you fellows have thought through a lot of things. But, now, how about some other aspects of the system?

Greg: What would you like to know?

Phil: How do you begin a session?

Greg: We usually start with what a counselee has written on our Personal Data Inventory (affectionately called the PDI). Rather than waste time during the counseling session gathering factual material (age, address, telephone number, etc.), we have counselees come half an hour before the first session to fill it out. Usually it takes about 20 minutes. In addition to those kinds of data, there are three questions at the end of the PDI with which we frequently begin: "What is the problem, as you see it?" "What have you done about it?" (an extremely important matter), and "What do you want us to do to help?"

Phil: I can see the importance of the first and the last questions, but I'm fuzzy about the second.

Greg: There are such things as *principal* problems (those that a person recognizes and that usually appear under question #1). But, often what he has done about it makes things worse. Those are *complicating* problems. Sometimes these are more serious than the original difficulty and must be dealt with before you can get to the principal problem. Often the counselee fails to recognize them.

Jane: And some of those complicating problems are brought on not only by the counselee's flawed attempts to extricate himself from a problem, but also by taking the advice of friends, or even of counselors who give unbiblical advice.

Greg: Exactly! And in response to the first question, we get three kinds of answers (the first two are the most common). Most often, there is a description of the problem that brought him to counseling (that is to say, whatever it was that irritated him or others enough to move him to seek help). A second level response – not as common as the first – has to do with the incident[s] that led to the problem expressed under the first question. Third, and least common, is the mention of a pattern possibly underlying the incident, one that has caused difficulty frequently in the past. If not corrected, this pattern of life will continue to crop up even after the current incidence of it is dealt with.

Let me show you what this is like by a very simple example: In answer to question one, the counselee writes, "I'm nervous all of the time." We will press further to discover what may lie behind this. Among other things, we might ask, "When did this nervousness begin?" He might say, "Around April 15th." We will then ask about his income tax return. If he admits to falsifying it, we can understand how that incident led to nervousness. Then we would probably ask, "Have you ever cheated on your tax return or in any other way that led to similar periods of nervousness?" Receiving a positive reply, we'd check out a few previous incidents to discover whether or not there is an underlying pattern that must also be dealt with. It will not be enough to square him off with the IRS this April. There may be other Aprils to handle, and other business incidents as well. So, you can see the importance of getting all of the facts. Answers on the PDI are usually of the first sort; we may have to probe for answers of the other types.

Phil: Wow! Nouthetic counselors do far more than I expected. But what about that question, "What do you want us to do to help?"

Jane: Can I answer that one?

Greg: Sure, go ahead.

Jane: If the person's goal is merely relief, then you have to show him that there is an even more important dimension. He must change his top goal in coming for counseling from relief to pleasing God! So the counselor must help him do so.

Greg: Very good, Jane.

Phil: I agree. Say, Jane, why don't we have supper some night this week and we can discuss these things some more?

Jane: Sounds good to me.

Greg: Are you telling me that you don't need to interview me further?

Jane & Phil: No, no!

Phil: But we can talk about the paper, the class, and the teacher's reaction that way better than here.

Greg: Hmmm. I see!

Phil: Let's set a time for the next interview. I can see that there's a lot more to nouthetic counseling than I realized.

Greg: Phil, this is *your* interview, about *your* paper. Do you want Jane to come back again?

Phil: Definitely!

Greg: Then we'll see you later on this week. Meanwhile, I'm going to give you a copy of a lecture I've been asked to deliver to some fledgling nouthetic counselors. It's entitled, "Why Nouthetic Counseling is Unique." By reading it you'll discover more of what you called the "mechanics" of nouthetic counseling [see Appendix A, page 139].

CHAPTER FIVE

[Phil and Jane arrive at the church early. Pastor Greg is just finishing the final six-week checkup session of a counseling case that has brought two estranged brothers in Christ together again.[1] Noticing the students from his study window, he asks Tom and Harry if they would like to say a word about their experience with nouthetic counseling. They heartily agree. As they enter, Phil and Jane are surprised to see these two men standing there.]

Greg: Phil and Jane, I'd like you to meet Tom and Harry, who have just completed a series of counseling sessions. I've asked them to say a word about their experience.

Phil: Great! I never expected to meet someone who has actually been through nouthetic counseling.

Jane: I'm delighted too!

Harry: Well, I don't know how much you know about nouthetic counseling, but I'll tell you one thing – it saved our relationship. When we came in here several weeks ago, we were at each other's throats. Now you can see we've worked that out biblically, and we are closer friends than ever.

Tom: You can say that again! And I want to emphasize one important fact – everything that happened was clearly backed up with Scripture. We didn't once hear Greg say, "I think this" or "I think that." Or "I suppose so." It was always, "God says."

Harry: We won't take any of your time now since you are here, as I understand it, to interview Greg. But if you ever want to talk to me in depth about what our experience was like, here's my business card – just give me a call and we'll set up a date to do so.

---

1. For information on the six-week checkup, see Jay E. Adams, *Three Critical Stages of Biblical Counseling*, Timeless Texts (2002).

Phil: Thank you. I just may do it.

Tom: I don't have a business card, but you can get my phone number and address from Pastor Greg if you need it. I would also be willing to help you any way I can.

Greg: Well, those spontaneous responses are quite gracious on your parts, I must say. Phil, I think that if you have the time, you ought to take Tom and Harry up on their offers.

Phil: If my school schedule permits, I'll do just that.

Jane: And you can count on me coming along.

Greg: That's first rate! Thanks Harry, Tom. We'll see you Sunday.

Tom & Harry: See you then. Goodbye and God's blessing on your paper.

[They leave and Phil and Jane take their seats.]

Phil: That surely was unexpected. Nice guys. It looks like I'm in the process of getting a thorough education in nouthetic counseling.

Greg: Nice guys *now*. But you should have seen them when they first came for counseling. Now, tell me, am I pushing too hard and fast?

Phil: No, no. How could I ask for more? This is splendid – I bet the rest of the students in our class won't have anything like this background for their reports!

Jane: Or a second interested person to help you out!

Phil: Jane's been a great help already. We really got into the paper thing on our supper date.

Greg: Date, eh? Sounds interesting!

Phil: Well, er, uh…I guess those words just slipped out. Sorry, Jane, if I misrepresented things.

Jane: I can tell you this – *I* considered it a date, and a good one at that!

Greg: It's interesting how nouthetic counseling brings people together, isn't it? OK, enough joshing around. Let's get down to business. Do you want to tell me anything about what you decided to do on your paper, or do you want to get right down to further questions about nouthetic counseling?

Phil: Well, there are a lot of decisions yet to be made about the report. I think we'll have to hold a couple more supper meetings to thrash them all out.

Jane: Yes. I expect he'll take me on a couple more nouthetic counseling *dates*!

Phil: OK, if you don't mind, I *certainly* don't mind calling them dates either, Jane.

Greg: So, you want to concentrate on issues, then? What is your first question?

Phil: There's one matter I want to get cleared up right away: The prof said that nouthetic counseling is wrong about forgiveness – that you don't believe it is to be given unconditionally. Jane took him on rather well, but I'd like to hear what you have to say about it.

Jane: I told him that it was like God's forgiveness of us, which is conditioned upon repentance and faith in Christ. Our forgiveness by God certainly is *not* unconditional, or everyone would be forgiven and saved.

Phil: But then he brought up the incident where the Amish girls were slain and the Amish community forgave the murderer unconditionally. It had to be so because the murderer committed suicide on the spot. We were a bit stumped by that one.

Greg: This is an important subject. Forgiveness is so important that if you don't understand the ins and outs, you will never be able to counsel effectively. Most cases that you will encounter, in one way or another, will require someone to ask for and someone to grant forgiveness. I'm going to have to tell you a number of things, but you can supplement them by reading Adams' book, *From Forgiven to Forgiving*. Now, let's get into a couple of basics. What is forgiveness?

Phil: Uh…ah…to accept a person's apology for a wrong he committed against you?

Greg: Wrong! Apologizing and saying you're sorry is the world's substitute for forgiveness.

Jane: I guess we goofed up on that one; I would have said the same thing as Phil. What is forgiveness then?

Greg: After you've scraped all else off, it boils down to this – forgiveness, at its heart, is *a promise*.

Phil: How's that? No one ever told me that.

Greg: In Ephesians 4:32 we are told that our forgiveness of one another is to be modeled after God's forgiveness of us. Now, what did God do when he forgave us? Did he get all mushy or something? Of course not! He said in Hebrews 10:17, "I won't remember their sins and their unrighteous deeds ever again." He went on record. He made a promise! He promised not to bring them up and use them against us in the future. God always keeps His promises, so we can be assured of His forgiveness. And that's the wonderful thing about our forgiveness of one another – when granted, one has made a promise that God expects him to keep. It's the only satisfactory way of settling matters. If the one who makes the promise doesn't keep it, *he* must repent and seek forgiveness. If he continues to violate his promise, church discipline may be necessary – but that's another story (and there's a complete book on that as well).

Jane: Wow! That's exciting. I think if we asked our prof what forgiveness is, *he* couldn't answer.

Greg: You might try it. I hope he's an affable enough person to reply. The Amish girls' slayer died unforgiven. Like the

Pharisees, he died "in [or with] his sins" (see John 8:21, 24). There was no opportunity for confession or forgiveness.

Now, you see, in apologizing, when one says "I'm sorry," the other person (after scraping his feet a bit) may say, "That's OK." But it really isn't. Why? Because no definitive transaction has taken place. No one asks for a promise, and no one gives one. Nothing is really settled. If a person confesses his sin against another and says, please forgive me, he is asking the other person to promise him not to remember it against him any more. If and when he makes that promise, a transaction, to which people can be held, has occurred. That's true biblical forgiveness.

Phil: The prof said that Jesus forgave people from the cross unconditionally.

Greg: But He didn't. That's either poor exegesis, or special pleading – or both! Jesus was praying to His Father, not granting forgiveness to those crucifying Him. By the way, do you think that God answered His Son's prayer?

Jane: I suppose God always answered Jesus.

Greg: OK. But how? [dead silence] No answer? Then, I'll tell you. He did so on the Day of Pentecost and thereafter when Peter and the apostles preached repentance and faith (conditions!) to that same crowd, and by the thousands those who were the subject of His prayer believed and were forgiven.

Phil: I get it! I see it! Forgiveness didn't occur *apart* from the means (preaching), but precisely *through* it.

Jane: And, it was conditional because they were not forgiven until they repented and believed the Gospel. Why didn't we figure that out? And why hasn't our prof done so?

Greg: Can't answer that one for sure, but perhaps it's because he spends too much time reading psychology texts and not enough studying his Bible. Now, there's much more to fully understanding the role of forgiveness in counseling that we can't begin to consider here, but you can read about it in

Adams' book if you care to. I just want to say two more things about it. First, forgiveness must take place whether we feel like it or not (cf. Luke 17:3ff.). Second, forgiveness is based on the naked word of the one saying, "I repent" (once again, refer to Luke 17). If his repentance is not genuine, and after several weeks of counseling there is no change, then it may be necessary to discover why there is no "fruit" of repentance (see Luke 3:8).

[Phil and Jane write down the verse in their notebooks.]

But only then. You cannot look into another's heart, as we saw. You can deal only with his words and works. At length, according to his final responses, you will have to treat him either as a believer or as a heathen and a publican.

Jane: So, I can see that there's a great deal to forgiveness in counseling, and that it *is* necessary to understand it to the full. I'm getting the book.

Phil: I'll borrow your copy! Or, better still [with a half smile that slowly creeps into a larger one], maybe we can read it together!

Greg: Now, this is getting just a little too thick, I'm afraid. Let's get on to the next topic.

Jane: I hate to break up the party, especially when it's getting so interesting, but my sociology class (ugh!) was changed and I'll have to leave now.

Phil: Well, I guess I'll go too. After all, it's my wheels that we're using.

Greg: So, we finish early today. But there's a great amount to think through concerning forgiveness. Hurry along. I'd hate to make you late. [Laughing.] And be sure you go directly to class!

Phil & Jane: [Also laughing.] We will, we will.

CHAPTER SIX

[Today, Phil and Jane arrive right on time. Pastor Greg and they exchange greetings and all sit down. The atmosphere is charged.]

Jane: We can't wait to tell you what happened!

Greg: What's that, Jane?

Phil: [breaking in] We talked to our professor, told him we had come to see you, how you graciously gave us time, and some of the things that were said. And he was interested.

Jane: He didn't seem upset at our explanations of nouthetic counseling – as we has supposed he might be. Indeed, everything that we told him, he said that he agreed with. The only difference, he claimed, is that he doesn't use the word "nouthetic" (he says the Greek word *paraklesis* is more appropriate) and that, otherwise, you both agree substantially about everything. You and he just use different language to describe the same things.

Greg: Well, that's most interesting. I wonder if he knows any Greek or if is he's just repeating what he's heard. Have you ever heard him mention Greek words before, or teach any of the things we've discussed, like the authority of Scripture, or the importance of forgiveness, or fulfilling your responsibilities even when you don't feel like it?

Phil: No. Come to think of it, can't say that I have.

Greg: Isn't that strange if he believes the same things? Why do you suppose that's so?

Phil: Well…perhaps, as he said, because he uses different terminology.

Greg: Can you fit any of what I have been telling you into his terminology? If what he says is true, I think you're clever enough to be able to make any translations necessary. But so much of what we've talked about seemed new to you Phil.

Jane: I'm sure we would be able to do so if what he said is correct. But *I* think his views and yours are actually antithetical rather than similar. As you know I've been arguing with him over much of what he's been teaching this semester. Somehow, his explanation doesn't seem kosher!

Greg: Did you show him the outline?

Phil: Yes, I did.

Greg: And what did he say about it? Did he agree with the fundamental presuppositions there?

Jane: No, I guess not. Come to think about it, he sort of passed it off as just one way to conduct a counseling session, but not necessarily the only one. And he indicated that it was nothing like his way. He thinks that there are many ways, I suppose, from what he said.

Greg: Does he actually do counseling, or only teach about it?

Phil: I don't know for sure, but I think he's just a teacher. At least, I've never heard that he does counseling, and in his lectures he never refers to any incidents that occurred during a counseling session. His lectures are all pretty general – and abstract. We never get down to the nitty-gritty.

Greg: Hmmmm. How did he handle the question as to what forgiveness is?

Jane: I know we asked him that, but I can't remember what his response was.

Phil: That's because he really didn't answer. You remember, Jane, he changed the subject.

Greg: Hmmmmm. All very interesting. And in some ways quite enlightening.

Phil: What are you thinking?

Greg: Of course, I can't judge his motives, and I surely don't know what is in his heart, but even from the sparse data you've provided, it seems that he acts and sounds like someone who doesn't want to face the issues. Sometimes, the easiest way to avoid conflict is to say that you agree, even when you don't. I certainly don't have any hard evidence for this; I'm just doing some preliminary – perhaps even wild – guessing. But there's something wrong somewhere, don't you think? While I don't want you to let my conjectures influence your thinking too heavily, you might look and listen to see if in any way they pan out in days to come.

Jane: Will do. The more I think about it, the more I realize that I learned little from the conversation – either about his own beliefs and methods or his genuine assessment of nouthetic counseling. All he talks about in class is classic counseling views. If we have the opportunity to speak again, I think I'll ask some more point-blank questions along those lines.

Phil: He did say that it might be nice sometime to have the four of us meet for lunch someplace to become better acquainted.

Greg: I'd welcome and enjoy doing so. Would it be just a social time, or would we talk shop? I suppose I could do either, but would prefer the latter. If you want to, and he is willing to follow up on his partial invitation, I'd be happy to have you set something up.

Jane: Great! We'll keep that in mind, and at the right time try to arrange such a meeting.

Greg: Just one more thing: the obvious dodge that many use when attempting to avoid the concept of *nouthesia* is to say that they prefer the Greek noun *paraklesis* (the verb is *parakaleo*) to describe counseling. Yet, that word is so large and all-encompassing that it is quite unacceptable as a defining term for counseling. It can mean to urge, comfort, console, encourage, appeal, exhort, counsel as a lawyer, and so on. Fundamental, as Souter says in his *Shorter Lexicon*, is that the paraklete is a "helper." To help is too general to specify a type of counseling.

Phil: That's interesting. I was surprised by his use of the word because I've never heard him mention it in class.

Greg: OK. Enough of that. Now let's get down to work. What did *you* think of the outline. I don't claim that it's the finest lecture outline in the world, but did it give you any new insights or raise any questions? It might be better to start with those matters, since they're probably fresh in your mind.

Jane: I have one observation: everything in it was so biblical, and so God-oriented. I was impressed with that above all else.

Phil: Jane commented to me about that, and said that if there was any overall feature that characterizes the whole, that was it. Just like Tom and Harry said. I was impressed with the way in which you emphasized that, ultimately, decisions and promises are made to God, not to the counselor. That puts just the right sort of pressure on the counselee to help him recognize the importance of how he responds to counseling.

Jane: I wondered when you wrote about the capabilities of the counselee to respond – in contrast to the non-Christian, non-counselee. Do believing counselees agree when you tell them that?

Greg: Not always. Often, when confronted with some difficult task – usually involving some sort of lifestyle change – a counselee might say, "Oh, I don't think that I could ever do that – or words to that effect. It's then that I must take time to reassure him that God has made him a new creature in whom His Holy Spirit dwells as Paul states in II Corinthians 6:16: "Now we are the temple of the living God." (You can also check out II Corinthians 5:17 and I Corinthians 2:10–16.) The Holy Spirit will grant him the wisdom and power he needs to do the difficult task before him. Then, I usually help him to look carefully at a verse or two (using too many confuses counselees), such as "I can do all things by Him Who strengthens me" (Philippians 4:13). Of course, Paul included in that very assuring sentence only those things that God wants us to do. And though he was speaking about living sparsely in that context, the principle Paul sets forth is larger than the context itself. There are other verses which might be used, that I am sure you can think of without me mentioning them. Sometimes people want to wait until they feel strong enough to act, but Jesus told the man with the withered hand to reach forth anyway, and strength to do so came in his obedient act of faith. James says that the blessing comes in the *doing* (James 1:25).

Phil: That's interesting, because it seems so much in accord with faith. Faith steps out on God's promises instead of basing an act upon a previously assured thing. It's probably best expressed by Paul's words, "We walk by faith, not by sight" (II Corinthians 5:7).

Greg: Now, of course, faith doesn't mean presumptuousness. First, one must be certain that what is proposed is truly God's command. Otherwise, he may go off half-cocked. I'm pleased that you saw the fact that God is central in every aspect of truly biblical counseling sessions. And, surely, faith plays a large part in the process. What else on the outline struck you or raised some question in your mind?

Phil: I have something. You note that the word translated "only-begotten" ought to be translated "unique." How come?

Greg: Good question. It was not until long after the King James version was published (1611 AD) that studies in the papyri showed that what had before seemed a contradiction to some was not really so. You see, we too were begotten (or born again) as children of God, so, in one sense Jesus isn't the *only begotten* Son. The studies showed that early translators assumed that "genes" in "monogenes" was from the root that meant "to beget offspring." Instead it was from the root that meant "to come into being" or "to exist." So, instead of "only-begotten," Jesus is actually declared to be the "unique" (or only-one-of-his-kind) Son. This, of course makes better sense.

Jane: I had another question. I didn't quite understand your distinction between methods and means. Can you elucidate?

Greg: Sure can. Means, as I was using the term, has to do with those capabilities that all of us have by virtue of being human: the ability to talk, to listen, to think, to plan, etc. Methods, on the other hand, are the use of those means to attain the desired ends (or goals) of a given system. A system of counseling is one in which a problem is defined in a certain way, leading to a defined solution. Then, means are developed that are consistent with one's view of a problem and its solution so as to move a counselee from the former to the latter. Methods are, in short, means committed to the ends of a system. Are you with me so far?

Jane: I think so. You're saying that a system requires the special use of means (which we all have at our disposal as human beings) to bring about desired results that are supposed to meet the requirements of some system.

Greg: Good. Let's illustrate. Skinner would never have used Rogers' methods, just as Rogers would never have used Skinner's. Why? Because they both thought very differently about man's basic problem. Those differences demanded that each would seek to attain quite different ends as their goals. Since Rogers believed that man comes into the world prepackaged with the answers to his problems, his goal was to get a counselee to look inside. So, he developed his reflective methodology. Skinner, on the other hand, believed man is only an animal and needed to be trained from the outside by reward and aversive control. Roger's methods, therefore were entirely unacceptable to Skinner. Skinner wanted to "train" counselees the way you train animals. So, his methods consisted of controlling them. Rogers, of course, would have none of that. If either used the others' methods successfully, he would reach ends exactly the opposite of the results that he desired!

Now, the point of all of this is that, in such things the "children of this world" are often smarter than those believers who naively think that they can attain the goals set forth in the Bible by methods eclectically borrowed from those whose methods have been designed to produce something quite different. Whether out of ignorance or laziness, the failure of eclectic Christians to develop truly biblical methods (a considerable task) leads them to attempt to integrate pagan methods into their counseling in order to attain biblical ends. But to do so is foolish and has proven unsuccessful. To obtain biblical results, one must begin with a biblical understanding of the problem, a biblical understanding of the solution to it, and then develop biblical methods that will lead from problem to solution. Get it?

Jane: I sure do! I knew all along that eclecticism was wrong, but I had a hard time stating why. I know now. Thanks.

Greg: You're welcome! Nouthetic counselors have spent years working out a biblical system. Naturally, much more could be said to expose the follies of eclectic thought and practice, but this may be enough for now. What else do you have for me?

Phil: When you spoke about results in the outline, the professor jumped on that and asked, "What scientific evidence do nouthetic counselors have for the superiority of their results? Can Greg show me any statistics from studies that have been made?"

Greg: Interesting question. There are several aspects to this matter. I'll mention just a few. Science can never prove or disprove anything about what goes on in the spiritual realm – it works exclusively with the physical world (if you mention social sciences, I simply discount much of what they do as soft rather than hard science, and therefore, disregard it as so much fluff).

Second, I have little confidence in most statistics, since I've studied and taught in academic institutions long enough to know that often there is great bias in the gathering, tallying and use of statistics in favor of conclusions already reached before testing. I also have known and read of sloppy work, and other work that was hurried up in order to reach deadlines.

But, all of that aside, the clincher is this: we don't believe in attempting to test the results of our counseling. Why? Because you can't put the Holy Spirit into a test tube, shake it and have Him turn out purple. That is to say, what we are dealing with is supremely what goes on in the inner life of a person – an area which cannot be tested. We can see and hear outward things, and sometimes make educated guesses; but they are never more than that. I can't tell for certain whether or not your faith is genuine; nor can you tell whether mine is. It's not our business to attempt to do so. God is the heart-Knower, who *alone* can test the heart. I already mentioned one verse, but here are some more to look up: see Acts 1:24; 15:8; I Corinthians 4:3–5; I Chronicles 29:17; Jeremiah 11:20.

The only way in which we test results is to determine whether or not the *counselor* has conformed to biblical standards in his counseling – not in the outward changes that are made in the *counselee*. Many seeds of spiritual change take time to germinate. What is said today may bear fruit only months later; what seems to bear fruit today may be short lived (the parable of the four soils is evidence for that).

Jane: That certainly is a viewpoint I hadn't considered. I thought nouthetic counselors had either neglected testing or didn't want to expose the results. But now I see you have a biblical rationale for rejecting them altogether.

Greg: Believe me, we are not copping out on this. Now, let me throw in one more comment. Suppose we did, in some way, test. The indicators we would use to measure success would be entirely different than what others would choose. We would determine counseling success if the counselee learned to honor God in his situation, if he abandoned relief as his uppermost goal and, as I said, if the counselor had properly ministered the Word even when it was unheeded. So, you see, we operate from very different standards – biblical ones – seemingly foolish and unacceptable to others (see I Corinthians 2). It would be comparing apples and oranges. Even if it were possible to test accurately (though, as I said, it isn't possible to judge spiritual things that way), we would only be ridiculed for what we call successes and failures because our standards for each are biblical and, therefore, unique.

Phil: I'm impressed! I had no idea that you had already thought through such matters, let alone could articulate them so fully.

Greg: There are other aspects of counseling that we are still investigating biblically, but I assure you there are many more that we have already settled.

Jane: It is getting late, and if we are going to go to class today we'd better be going.

Phil: You're right. Can we come again? My paper is shaping up and I want to be sure I have matters accurately stated. I'm not asking you to read it, but I may have some more questions after Jane and I peruse the material further.

Greg: Certainly. I'll be glad to meet with you as often as necessary, but don't feel any necessity to come. Next time I'd like to take up the flawed mantra of the eclectics who chant, "All truth is God's truth" and, that therefore, we must accept truth revealed through Freud, et al. And, by the way, you may tell your professor that I accept his invitation – and I'll pay!

[Both Jane and Phil leave for class, with ammunition under their arms – namely the profuse notes they have been taking.]

CHAPTER SEVEN

[Jane and Phil are talking vigorously as they come down the hall toward the church study. Greg, hearing their animated discussion, wonders what is happening. They enter.]

Greg: Well, good to see you.

Jane: You won't believe what happened!

Phil: Yeah!

Jane: We told Professor Burns that you had accepted his invitation, and he turned you down!

Phil: Now, wait a minute. It wasn't exactly like that. He said that he was too busy at the moment. So, I asked him when it might be convenient to get together, and he blurted out, "I don't think that I want to get together with Dawson; all he'll do is criticize everything I say."

Jane: I told him that I had found you a very reasonable person who was genuinely interested in arranging the lunch in order to meet him. I then explained that you said you'd be willing to make it purely social or a time to talk shop – whatever he wished. But he just turned and went about his business without a reply.

Greg: Was there anything else that you did or said that might have led him to believe what he said? Jane, you often challenged his views in class. Do you think that he believes I've been putting you up to it?

Jane: I can't see how that could be so. He knows that neither of us had ever met you before Phil made the appointment to interview you about his paper. I don't understand what's gotten into him. He's always been cordial before. I am pretty sure that we couldn't have triggered this reaction by anything that we did or said.

Greg: How do you see it, Phil? Do you think that your paper will be in jeopardy because of this unfortunate exchange?

Phil: I agree with Jane. I doubt that we said anything to cause this response. And – about the paper – I haven't the faintest idea what he might do about it, if anything. I can't see how we could be threatening to him, though it *seems* that he's afraid to talk with you.

Greg: That's regrettable. I hope I haven't caused you any difficulty at school. I would have enjoyed meeting him, and especially – if he agreed – talking to him about our differences. I know that we could have pulled it off in a relaxed, Christian manner. I think that we should pray about the whole matter, don't you?

Jane & Phil: Yes!

[Greg prays. He asks God's blessing upon the efforts of Phil and Jane to learn the truth about biblical counseling, and that He will help Phil do well on his paper. Moreover, he prays that God will soften Professor Burns' heart and make him willing to meet sometime in the future after all – if He so wills.]

Greg: Please give my warmest regards to the professor the next time you have an opportunity to speak to him, and tell him I greatly regret the fact that we could not meet at this time, but that I understand how pressing academic responsibilities can be. Tell him I was looking forward to the time together with great anticipation and that I hope sometime in the future we will be able to meet. Then drop the matter.

Now, I think we were going to talk about the integrationist's slogan, "All truth is God's truth." Under that rubric, all sorts of wrong, harmful ideas from non-Christian systems of counseling have been imported into the church. For instance, one Christian counselor propagates the views of Adler. And it's handy for him and others, if called to task for doing so, to quote the slogan. The mere quotation of it is supposed to bring the discussion to an end.

Usually, this slogan goes along with an explanation that God reveals much through unbelievers by means of "general revelation." The problem with that, however, is that while God does reveal Himself in nature through creation, there is no biblical warrant for thinking he uses men like Adler to reveal truth. There isn't the slightest indication of that sort of revelation in the Bible. Historically, what theologians have called general revelation is the kind of data mentioned in Romans 1 and Psalm 8. Now, what can be determined from such revelation is that there is a Creator and that we, as sinners, are in trouble with Him. As important as those truths are, that's about the sum of it. Even salvation is not revealed through nature – let alone truth about how to counsel! It's by "special revelation" (today found in the Bible alone) that we learn about Christ and redemption, as well as those counseling facts that are, in essence, elements of sanctification. Even the minor amount of general revelation which God gives us, He says sinners suppress (Romans 1:18). To toss in all sorts of ideas under the rubric of general revelation is an unbiblical construct. Of course, all truth *is* God's truth; the saying is a truism. And a correlative truism is "All error is the devil's error!" How do we distinguish the two? The question boils down to this: how does *God* say that He reveals truth to man?

The crucial fact to note when speaking of revelation is this: all revelation from God is perfect, inerrant. What Adler discovered, if anything, is not revelation at all. At best, it is merely human discovery. But nothing – I repeat – *nothing* is perfect and inerrant except that which God truly reveals. All "human discoveries" are deficient and often quite erroneous. Scientists know this and are constantly correcting their understandings of "discoveries." Though integrationists like to sling the word revelation around, there isn't a shred of evidence that any psychologist or psychiatrist could substantiate the claim that divinely-revealed truth was given to him. All men err – psychologists, perhaps, more than many others! Anything they say is tainted by sin and always contains error. Why would a Christian want to trade a perfect, written revelation from God – designed to provide all things necessary for life and godliness – for the error-ridden ideas of men? Because of the noetic effects of sin (how sin has affected man's thinking), we can *expect* him to lean in wrong directions. And, what is true of Christians – who also are far from perfect – is doubly true of those who have no basis in true revelation from which to do their thinking.

Phil: Wow! I've heard that slogan over and over, and I didn't know what to think of it. But don't these men have some truth? What of common grace?

Greg: Nothing that can be called truth in any rightful sense of the word. Pure, unadulterated truth is found only in what God reveals. He alone knows all things past, present, and future in relation to all other things, and such comprehensive knowledge as that is necessary for truth. Otherwise, some facts might be missed that would change everything. No human being has comprehensive knowledge. Ours is miniscule and tainted, at best. We can claim, however, to know truth through the Bible, though it isn't comprehensive. How? Because it is revealed by God out of His comprehensive knowledge, and given to us in a form that is intelligible to those in whom His Spirit dwells. And the only thing that keeps us from distorting revelation more than we do is the Holy Spirit within. Even then, because of our old ways, we still distort truth. But if our starting point is truth that God has revealed, we can begin our thinking much closer to reality than those who depend upon the "wisdom" of others who err like themselves. And we always may return to Scripture for the Holy Spirit's correction of our errors. We begin from inerrant revelation rather than from the "wisdom" of others who have no idea of the source of truth. We think from inerrant revelatory presuppositions and principles rather than errant human "discoveries" and men's interpretations of them. And, as for common grace, there is also much wrong thinking. What is common to believers and unbelievers alike is not God's grace but His goodness – sending rain on the fields of both, restraining sinners from becoming any worse than they are, and the like. The Bible knows nothing of some sort of common grace *revelation*.

Jane: That's awesome!

Greg: Pardon me for suggesting this, but why don't you reserve the term awesome for God alone?

Jane: Gotcha!

Greg: For a larger discussion of this matter, you can read Adams' book, *Is All Truth God's Truth?*

Phil: I suspect that in time I will. But for now, I think to take on too much would destroy my paper. I plan to reserve much information in the back of my head, however, for the Q&A period following the report on my paper. You see, the class-room report is to be a kind of long abstract of the paper itself.

Greg: Now, what else do you want to discuss at this time?

Jane: I'd like to ask a question. Do you think that Phil should proselytize in his paper? I mean, should he try to convert some of the students to nouthetic counseling?

Greg: No. I'd advise that his presentation should be cool, factual, and very objective. I don't think that he should do any such thing *in class*. If he presents the matter convincingly, but non-polemically, he'll probably have students come to him after class to discuss it further. Then he'll have plenty of opportunity to convince them. However, since there will be a Q&A period following the reading of the report abstract, that may provide an opportunity to gently refute some errors. In general, he should be as wise as serpents and gentle as doves.

Phil: Good advice! I'll take it to heart.

Greg: Not mine – it's Christ's. Now, what more do we need to talk about today?

Phil: Actually, I want to cut the discussion short and spend the rest of my time preparing for the term paper and the class report. What I'd like to do, if you're agreeable, is to meet the next time after the report to discuss what took place and then, from time to time, continue to meet simply to discuss nouthetic counseling itself – apart from any need to prepare for a class presentation. I'm interested to learn all that I can. I can get most of the material that I still need from Adams' *Christian Counselor's Manual,* his *Theology of Counseling,* and his *How to Help People Change.* What I'd like to do after the report is to look into my own future with you. I've been considering becoming a nouthetic counselor myself, so I need to know all that involves.

Greg: Sounds sensible to me. I would be delighted, and consider myself privileged, to help you through your decision. But remember, I'm going to stress the ministry of the Word when I do so.

Phil: I think I understand where you're coming from, and I want to examine the ins and the outs of the matter. One thing I know now, I am going to drop my psychology major for a Greek or Bible major. I no longer see a place for so-called Christian psychology. Actually, I've come to see that there isn't any such thing as "Christian psychology" anyhow.

Greg: Jane, will you be coming with Phil in the future?

Jane: You can count on it! There's a lot more going on here now between us than our interest in nouthetic counseling – although that is still very important to me. Nouthetic counseling, as you once noted, has been bringing us together!

Greg: Good. It will be interesting to see how close you become. And, if it should ever reach that point, I'd be glad to show you how a nouthetic counselor does premarital counseling!

Jane: Cool!

CHAPTER EIGHT

[It's two weeks later. Today is the day that Phil is to give his report to the class. Greg wonders how it will go, and prays that God will give him clarity of thought and faithfulness in presenting it. He also prays that Phil's fellow students and Professor Burns will receive what they hear with open hearts and minds. He wonders, too, how Jane is doing. It surely would be great for God to call Phil into the ministry and Jane to become his wife. But that's God's business, and Greg knows that while he might be of help to them in making the decision, he must not push it. He is now waiting for word from this fine young couple, since they promised to call him as soon as the "ordeal" was over. The phone rings; it's Jane.]

Jane: Pastor Greg, we've just got to see you as soon as possible!

Greg: Sure. I'll be available this evening, if you want to come to my home.

Jane: I don't know if this can wait. Do you think that you would have time right now?

Greg: Well, I'm only studying for a lecture I have to give, and I think that it can wait a while.

Jane: Good. I'll be right over.

Greg: Wait a minute. What about Phil? Isn't he coming?

Jane: No. At least not now. I'll explain when I come.

Greg: OK. See you soon.

[This sounds strange – Jane excitedly calling and Phil not coming. Something, it seems, has gone wrong. I need to ask God to help me handle whatever it may be, and to bless this young couple. He does. Twenty minutes later Jane arrives, red faced from rushing, still puffing as she takes her seat.]

Jane: You can't imagine what happened!

Greg: That's for sure! Please tell me.

Jane: Well, Phil gave his paper and then it all exploded!

Greg: Oh? Exactly what happened?

Jane: It was a good paper. Perhaps the best offered in class this semester. Phil had worked diligently to make it so. He was cool and non-aggressive. And it seemed to go over well. It was afterwards, during the discussion that it all broke loose! You see, there's a very brilliant member of our class – perhaps the smartest. Brian Wishart is his name – and he started it all.

Greg: Come on Jane, get to the point; I'm dying to hear.

Jane: Well, Brian got up and looked Prof Burns squarely in the eye and said, "You're a fraud! Here you are in a Christian college supposedly teaching us Christian psychology and you haven't said a thing all semester that even begins to approximate with what we've just heard! What Phil has said is biblical. Why haven't we been hearing this in class? I feel that I've been cheated!"

Greg: Oye! What happened then?

Jane: Well, Burns got burned up (excuse the pun). He stammered and he wheezed and got red around the neck. I thought he was going to burst a blood vessel. But Brian – who is known as a brain around school (but not a nerd) – wouldn't let up. He went on and on in the same vein, and finally marched out of the room saying, as he left, "I'm going to see the dean about this, and if I don't get satisfaction there, I intend to see a lawyer!" Or, words to that effect.

Greg: Ohhhh!

Jane: And you can count on him doing what he says. His father was on the board, and is a major contributor to the University.

Greg: Where's Phil?

Jane: He's trying to cool Brian down. He headed after him when everything went to pieces and half of the class stormed out. He's concerned not only for the testimony of nouthetic counseling – but for Brian and Burns as well! If things go Brian's way, Burns could be in real trouble. And if things go the other way – yikes! There goes Phil!

Greg: Well, before we do anything more, let's pray. Jane, since you know the facts, why don't you lead us in prayer? [Jane does.]

Greg: Now, where do you think that Brian and Phil might be?

Jane: That's hard to tell. If they aren't in one of their dorm rooms, then they're probably sitting in the Bluebird Café across from the dorms.

Greg: Well, let's call around and see if we can locate them. Do you know the number of the dorm?

Jane: Sure. I'll call. [After several minutes of unsuccessfully trying to reach them, Jane and Greg decide to take a look in the Bluebird, which is also one of Greg's favorite snack shops.]

CHAPTER NINE

[As they enter the Bluebird, sure enough, they spot Phil and Brian sitting at a table in the back of the room vigorously discussing matters with one another. The two approach, unnoticed.]

Phil: You've gotta take it easy on Burns, I tell you, Brian. The poor guy just hasn't had the proper education to teach counseling. He's been trained in psychology, not in the Bible.

Brian: Obviously! But isn't that the point? Why do we have to put up with such stuff in a Christian institution?

Phil: Granted, we shouldn't have to, but...[Phil sights Jane and Greg standing there listening]. Oh, here's Greg now. Brian, let me introduce you two. You know Jane, of course. This is Pastor Greg Dawson, who provided a lot of helpful information for my paper.

Greg: Glad to meet you Brian. Do you mind if we join you? I could use a snack, how about you Jane?

Jane: Couldn't if I were starving; I'm too engrossed!

Brian: Happy to meet you, the man who helped set things straight in our class!

[The waitress comes. "What'll you have?"]

Greg: I'll take a personal cheese pizza, and water to drink.

Jane: All I need is water, thanks. Now, fellows, where has this gotten to?

Brian: The basic issues about nouthetic counseling are settled so far as I'm concerned. We need to teach it at Christian U. But about Prof Burns – what *are* we going to do?

Phil: I keep telling you, it's the school's fault for hiring someone who has his credentials. He's not to blame for teaching exactly what he was hired to teach.

Brian: I know that. But, still, you'd think, that as a Christian who's smart enough to earn a Ph.D., he'd be able to figure things out for himself.

Phil: Teachers like him have a doctor's degree in psychology and a Sunday School degree in Bible. They just haven't a clue. Besides, what I said in my paper challenges the validity of his position and his future.

Greg: Guys, I know that this was a difficult day for you, but let's see if we can pull something constructive out of it.

Jane: Such as?

Greg: Sorry Jane. By "guys" I didn't mean just Phil and Brian. I didn't mean to leave you out. I was using "guys" generically – or something like that.

Jane: I understood – but what can we *do* about the mess?

Greg: Well, I'd like to begin by nouthetically confronting Brian. Tell me, was what you did in class right?

Brian: Everything I said was true.

Greg: I didn't ask about what you said; only about what you did.

Brian: Well...nooo; I guess not. I did raise quite a ruckus. I should have handled things better. It just got the better of me hearing...ah...come to think of it, I guess you're right! What I did *was* over the top.

Greg: So, if you want to be biblical, you will seek Professor Burns' forgiveness – and also the forgiveness of the class for the way that you acted.

Brian: Tell him I'm sorry?

Greg: No, ask God and him for forgiveness. I'm going to give you a book called *The Case of the "Hopeless Marriage"* (I have a copy in my car), and I want you to read it before class tomorrow. It's not that long, and it's easy reading. In it you'll discover the difference between biblical forgiveness and apologizing. I know, after what you said, you'll certainly want to do the biblical thing – right?

Brian: Uhh…I guess so. Uhh…No, you're right. I do want to do the biblical thing.

Greg: Good. Getting that settled, we can move on to what you *said*.

Brian: Yeah! That's the important thing.

Greg: No. It's *all*-important. Truth is critical; but how you express it can make all the difference between its acceptance and its rejection. You may have set nouthetic counseling back a generation among the members of your class and in that school – not to mention the effect it had on Dr. Burns.

Brian: Yeah. Well…I guess you're right about that. But *what* I said was the truth!

Greg: Was it? *All* of it?

Brian: Sure! A Christian university ought to present Christian truth about every subject – including what God says about man. Why Burns hasn't cracked a Bible all semester!

Greg: Is that all you said?

Brian: Uhh…Mmmm. O, I guess I did go a bit too far in calling him a fraud. I suppose he's doing what he believes he ought to do, acting on his best understanding – which is unequivocally wrong!

Greg: Right. Think you ought to say something about that in your confessions to him and the class when you seek forgiveness?

Brian: Yeah, you're right. Nouthetic counseling isn't always so easy, I guess. Here I am trying to defend it in class, and on the other hand hesitant to act in accordance with its biblical principles! OK, I'll handle it tomorrow. Let's get that book. I've got some serious reading to do tonight.

[Brian and Greg leave to go to the car for the book. As they do, Greg says,] I'll be right back. We need to talk some more. You have some repair work to do too!

Jane: What could he mean? We didn't do anything.

Phil: Maybe that's the problem. Perhaps we should have done something.

Jane: I guess we shouldn't have walked out with Brian.

Phil: And I think we might have poured oil on troubled waters. We could have said something to forestall the final blowup.

Greg: Right! I suppose you didn't hear us return.

Jane: When you say "right," to what are you referring?

Greg: For one thing, pouring that oil. For another, trying to calm Brian down. And, certainly, refusing to join the exodus Brian led.

Phil: I can see that now. So, we also have some apologiz...I mean *confessing of sin* to do, too?

Jane: I certainly do. You'd think as the feminine member of the trio causing all of the trouble I'd at least have known to speak softly...

Phil: While carrying a big stick? Hmmmmmm. I'm going to have to look into this farther if I ever come to the place where our relationship gets thicker.

Greg: It's a good thing you said that with a smile on your face!

Jane: You'd better believe so! I might stage another walk out!

Greg: Hey! Wait a minute. Let's leave that till later; this is serious business.

Phil: OK, OK. Now, how are we going to handle matters?

Jane: Do you have any ideas, Pastor Greg?

Greg: I think what you've suggested so far is right. You might also meet and pray with Brian before class tomorrow. By the way, you didn't go to the dean, did you Brian?

Jane: No. Remember, I got to you before he could do anything more. After they stomped out, he and Phil went immediately to the Bluebird to talk.

Greg: Good. Brian, you'd have been in no mood to talk properly to the dean. There might come a time, not too long from now, when the three of you do sit down with the dean or the president of the school and have a quiet talk about the curriculum. But that can wait until you've done all you can to rectify the damage done. Notice, there has been damage; but confession, seeking forgiveness, and trying to help all concerned isn't damage-control of the sort politicians practice. What I'm talking about is true heart-felt repentance. To be meek is not to be weak. Indeed, it is one evidence of strength. To handle difficult situations and people well without violating any of Jesus' commands about love is meekness in action. Remember, the meek will inherit the earth! Perhaps you can lay claim to at least a bit at the University. This altercation can be turned to good, if handled God's way!

Phil: That's certainly what I want.

Jane: Me too!

Greg: Let's pray about tomorrow, asking God to use your confessions to raise (not lower) the status of biblical counseling! [They pray.]

Greg: Let me know what happens!

Jane, Phil & Brian: We will!

CHAPTER TEN

[The next day Greg gets a phone call from Phil.]

Phil: Pastor Greg. I'd have come as soon as possible, but something is going on here that I simply can't walk out on.

Greg: What's up?

Phil: Class has just ended, and what a time we had! We did everything that you said to do – Brian, Jane and I – and we're still at it. Most of the members of the class stayed for further discussion. Prof Burns is in the thick of it. He's been pretty good about it, given what went on. And everyone wants you to come right over and join in the discussion. Can you come?

Greg: Well, Phil, I'd like to but I'm about to meet with a counselee any minute now, and we'll be at least an hour or so. Sorry. I'd like to help, but can't right now.

Phil: I understand, but everyone will be disappointed.

Greg: Is there another time we could get together? I don't want anyone to think that I'm wimping out.

Phil: Well, I don't think that we'd be able to get the whole class and Burns together again. Perhaps, in God's providence it just wasn't to be.

Greg: I'm afraid that you and Jane will have to hold your own.

Phil: OK. I understand. We'll do our best. Pray for us.

Greg: Will do. [Phone call ended, Greg prays immediately for the meeting. One hour later Jane phones.]

Jane: Pastor Greg, has your counseling session ended?

Greg: Just did. It was a productive session. How did things go with you, Phil and Brian?

Jane: Things are still going! In fact, I'm calling for the group. We'd all like to come over to the church and meet with you in your study. I assured them that you'd agree if you didn't have another appointment. Hope I wasn't too forward.

Greg: Not at all. But let me get this straight – everyone's coming here? Now?

Jane: That's the idea; we had to give up the classroom for another graduate class. How about it?

Greg: Wonderful! I'll look forward to the meeting. When can I expect you all?

Jane: I'd say in about three quarters of an hour. Let's see, there should be Phil and Brian and I and Prof Burns and Milt and Bob and Dawn. Altogether, I count seven. Is that OK?

Greg: Good. It's just fine with me. Possibly God has provided something even better for us than if I had come to the school earlier. We'll not be pushed out here. I'll be waiting. [Greg calls the local pizza shop orders four large pizzas, six bottles of root beer and three dozen donuts, which the pizza shop also sells. He says to himself, "This could be pretty exciting. A little snack ought to help calm everyone down." Greg then leans back in his office chair and awaits the food and the crowd.]

CHAPTER ELEVEN

[The Pizza truck is just pulling out of the church driveway when a procession of four cars drives in. "Perfect timing," Greg thinks. "Here they come. Lord, this is an opportunity; help me to make the most of it for your sake!" Greg goes out to meet them as they arrive at the church door. Greetings are exchanged all around, and it's evident that everyone is anxious to get on with the discussion. Greg tries to be especially friendly to Professor Burns, at whose side he leads the crowd through the hall to his study. He thinks, "I'm sure glad that I convinced the elders of the church to provide a study large enough for a gathering of this sort!" Extra chairs are brought in from a Sunday School room across the hall, and everyone is soon seated comfortably in what roughly approximates a circle.]

Greg: You're all welcome. Have some grub while it's still hot. I thought some of you might need a little food to fortify you at this late hour in the afternoon. I can't tell you how honored I am that you all came – especially that *you* wanted to accompany the class, Professor Burns.

Prof. Burns: These aren't the greatest circumstances under which to make your acquaintance, but I'm glad to meet you anyway.

Greg: Well, I'm hoping that the circumstances will improve before our discussion is completed. Unavoidably, I've missed most of the discussion thus far. Could anyone bring me up to speed?

Prof. Burns: I'll start; then anyone else who wants to may fill in the gaps.

Greg: Excellent!

Prof. Burns: As you undoubtedly know, we had quite a ruckus yesterday. Phil gave his paper – a well-written one I must say; then Brian jumped up and began to charge that I was a fraud, that the school was remiss in offering psychology instead of biblical counseling – whatever that is – and threatened to consult with the dean and/or bring the law into the matter! I can tell you that it was not a pleasant experience. I'm afraid that I lost my cool and said a few things in response that I now regret.

Brian: So did I, and so do I.

Prof. Burns: Well, at any rate, I went home and talked it all over with my wife, who is a fine Christian, and always gives me sound spiritual advice. She said that she thought the class – and Brian in particular – was very wrong to act as they did, but suggested that I give some cool, calculated thought and prayer to *what* was said. "Forget the dust up," she said. "Think about the content of the remarks made, and the paper that incited them. Who knows, perhaps the Lord has a purpose in what took place, that will be a blessing to all involved." Well I did, and I must say that Brian's words (not his attitude) were a challenge to me. I couldn't help but wonder whether there wasn't *something* to them. We are a Christian university. So, I asked God to show me if there is something to learn from what took place.

Well, I didn't look forward to this afternoon's class, I can assure you. But I went with as open and kindly a spirit as I could muster. I suppose it wasn't what it ought to be by any means, but I decided to confront the class in a Christian attitude to see what would come of it. But before I could get three words out of my mouth, Brian got to his feet and asked if he could say something. I thought, "Oh boy, here it comes – another tirade!" But it wasn't. Politely, he asked for my forgiveness for his attitude, only to be followed by others who sought forgiveness for walking out, etc. I was startled, to say the least. Wondering what had come over them, I asked, "What happened to change you so radically?" "Well," Brian said, "We were confronted nouthetically" – I think those were his words – "about our attitudes, especially mine. Now will you please forgive me?" You could have knocked me over with a cue-tip, but I recouped and said, "I will, but we can't have any more outbursts like that. There can be no learning where there is animosity and chaos." Phil broke in and conceded that this was true. Jane explained that they had gone to see you and that you had dealt with them rather firmly. I can only thank you for that!

Phil: Then, we asked Dr. Burns if we could talk matters over calmly and express opinions on all sides. He agreed, and – well, here we are two-and-a-half-hours later – still talking.

Brian: Since I was the chief instigator I guess it falls on me to say a thing or two first. Unless you have more to say, Dr. Burns.

Prof. Burns: No, not now. But I reserve the right to do so later if necessary.

Brian: Well, Pastor Greg, we've spent the lion's share of our time discussing whether or not psychology is the best training one could receive for counseling. We don't know too much about other options, but at least we've been able to begin to take a hard look at that abstract question itself.

Milt: What some of us have concluded so far is that at the very least there might be some sort of integration between Bible and psychology – right Bob? To teach straight out that psychology is the answer to men's problems is certainly not a *Christian* approach. If our salvation was provided by Christ, will he leave us now that we're saved and do no more?

Bob: I agree. Some sort of blending seems necessary. The issue that we haven't been able to resolve is whether one particular psychology is what ought to be blended with Scripture truth or whether a more eclectic approach would be better. However, on the other side, one question that came up was, "Why would God leave the church helplessly floundering until Freud and those who followed came along?" Seems like a long time to wait for answers, and lots of Christians left without the help they need, if psychology is necessary.

Dawn: Yes, in line with that is the other approach that radically differs from either the integration or the eclectic ones. I think that Jane (and probably Phil and Brian) believe that counseling psychology is a harmful substitute for the Scriptures. They see no place for it.

Brian: You're right. I've just about reached that conclusion.

Phil: I'm definitely of that opinion.

Jane: And you can include me too.

Dawn: So, you see we're at odds on a most fundamental matter. It would seem that if we can't settle that we'll make little progress, and we'll have to go away agreeing to disagree.

Prof. Burns: You can understand my reticence to go along with your views. After all I've invested a number of years in studying and teaching psychology, and I'm sure it has helped many. There is so much that psychology has to offer that can't be found in the Bible. I could possibly entertain some sort of integration, but to eliminate psychology from counseling – that's too much!

Jane: Well, that's about it, Pastor Greg. That's how matters stand. What have you got to say about the matter? Can you help us?

Greg: First, let's be thankful for good Christian wives like Professor Burns' wife! And for the Bible to bring us up short when we act wrongly. As to the issues you've presented, I have more to say than I could possibly mention this evening. But perhaps we can at least get our teeth into it a bit. Speaking of teeth – go ahead and finish the food. It may take some time to even begin to explain things. Any such far-reaching decision demands a lot of time and thought. So, why don't I make a few preliminary remarks, and then sit back and see how they grab you. Is that OK?

Prof. Burns: It is with me. I'm anxious to hear what your side (if I can call it such) has to say.

[The rest agree that Greg should make some sort of initial statement about the matter so that they could better understand his position and discuss it more intelligently.]

Greg: OK, then. You have all heard Phil's paper. I haven't heard or seen it myself, but in providing some source material for him, I gather he must have rather accurately – though not fully – presented the nouthetic counseling position. Fundamentally, it's this: Every counseling problem is at heart a theological problem. Every counseling solution is at heart a theological solution. And the theology that Christians should always adopt is a Bible-centered one. That is to say, we believe that in the Scriptures God has provided "everything" we need to know "for life and godliness." That statement is found in II Peter 1:3. It means that everything a person needs to inherit eternal "life," and to live in a "godly" way, pleasing to Him, is found in the Scriptures. The assertion boils down to this: there is no substitute, or need to supplement, those things that have to do with either salvation or sanctification. *All* the truths needed to live for Christ are found in the Scriptures. I think we would all agree about salvation – that there's no other way to be saved than by Jesus Christ, and that all one needs to know to be saved can be found in the Scriptures. [There are some verbal and non-verbal assents.] So, it's only when we get to the second half of Peter's proposition that our thinking diverges. Nouthetic counselors believe that just as his statement about salvation ("life") is absolute and exclusive, so too is his statement about sanctification ("godliness" – a life pleasing to God). Are you with me so far?

[One or two respond, "What you say is clear enough," or words to that effect]

Greg: Good. Now, understand that the matters that fall under sanctification – being set apart *from* sin and *for* God – encompass all counseling situations, because they all have to do with living life in relation to other people (one's self, other human beings and God). We believe that this is the stuff of which counseling is made. You don't go for counseling in order to learn how to fix your computer, but you do go for help in how to fix your marriage. Counseling deals with loving God and one's neighbor.

Prof. Burns: Ah! Then, there *are* things that you need to do for which the Bible doesn't have answers.

Greg: Good point. Of course there are. You see, the Bible does indicate we should avail ourselves of the expertise of non-Christians in things that don't pertain to interpersonal relations. For instance, David and Solomon properly sought the help of Hiram, a pagan, when they needed expert builders and other craftsmen. They didn't go to him, however, for help about how to improve relations among their subjects.

Prof. Burns: So, you distinguish between those things that you say a counselor concerns himself with and other matters. Seems to me a bit limiting.

Greg: Well, later on, when we pursue this matter in depth, I'd like to discover from you what it is that a psychologist does that a Christian counselor shouldn't do? I'd very much like to hear your response.

Prof. Burns: Right now, just to throw one matter on the table, I'd say, "Deal with mental illness."

Greg: The term is one that we think wrongly describes a person's problems unless he is speaking of a truly physical difficulty. I mean, like the one that occurs when you hit him over the head with a crowbar. We find that there's no such thing in the Bible as a non-organic "illness." In fact, as we see it, the term is an oxymoron. By the way, your training would be purely academic, I assume. Unlike a psychiatrist – who has medical credentials – you are no more qualified to deal with an "illness" than we are. Right?

Prof. Burns: Well, you see, mental illness is different.

Greg: How? If it's truly an illness, it must be organic. The term is accurate only if truly defining a bodily or physical sickness. We only use the word "illness" metaphorically when, for instance, we speak of relationships between people as "sick." If the conditions misnamed "mental illness" aren't organic, then they are no different from other poor relationships, which are not illnesses but problems in living. Thomas Szass, a prominent psychiatrist, wrote a book entitled, *The Myth of Mental Illness.* And a number have followed his lead. In fact, a large proportion of the psychiatric world has come to see this fact.

Prof. Burns: Go on. We can get into this again later. I can see it's going to take us more than this one discussion to do so.

Greg: OK. Now, as I was saying, the Bible is adequate even for dealing with non-personal problems in that, by both precept and example, it encourages us to turn to non-Christians for help in those things about which it offers no instruction. But, when it comes to matters of living in relation to God, to one's neighbor and to one's self, it has much to say – in fact, as Peter made clear, "everything" we need. After all, the sum of the law and the prophets is data on how to love God and one's neighbor. And, there is nothing necessary about that which it omits. So, since psychology covers the same ground as nouthetic counseling, we see no need to incorporate anything from the outside into our counseling – either having to do with "theory" [Greg makes quotation marks with his fingers] or practice. I'm simply using the word "theory" to help you understand – we believe God's teaching and requirements are more than mere theory; they are nothing less than truth.

Milt: You're saying, then, that integration and eclecticism are both taboo? You see no place whatsoever for integration of biblical and non-biblical truth?

Greg: Precisely. Except that we cannot call non-biblical views about counseling "true."

Dawn: But isn't all truth God's truth?

Greg: That slogan certainly is true. But it's also correct to say that, "All error is the Devil's error." So, the question arises as to how the two may be distinguished. Only Scripture can do so. Again, psychology is deficient in this regard. Moreover, in dealing with truth there is no shred of agreement among psychotherapists: there are, conservatively speaking, 250 different types of psychology and psychotherapy in the USA alone. Some count a much higher number. Moreover, as I told Phil – by the way, Phil did you deal with this matter in your paper...?

Phil: Yes, I did.

Greg: Then you know, Dawn, that God alone is the Source of truth, and that He reveals His truth through the Bible. He reveals no truth through Freud, Rogers, Skinner, Adler, et al. We know this since none of them is infallible; none has given us absolute, inerrant truth; and God has not told us to seek truth from them. On the other hand, everything God reveals in the Bible is absolutely true. I probably don't have to go into this more fully, since I suspect his paper "Philed" in the details! [groans] What psychologists and psychiatrists supposedly have "discovered" is nothing more than that – human discovery. And all such is subject to rejection, modification, substitution, etc. Unlike Scripture, it is neither inerrant, unchangeable, nor absolute. To put it simply – it isn't revelation.

Dawn: I guess I do remember that part of his paper now that you remind me, but – at the time – it seemed so far-fetched that I simply passed it off.

Greg: Sometimes, it's better to get it firsthand, in a different context. Now let me go on. Let's take up a subject like depression.

Prof. Burns: That's one I'd like to hear. Don't tell me you deal with depressed people too!

Greg: Yes, we certainly do. And successfully. Let me say just a few of the many things I could say about depression to give you an idea of how we counsel depressed people. First, we don't believe it is an illness. So we don't deal with it as such. If we are correct, then those who think of it as an illness from

64

the outset head in the wrong direction. One's view of the problem will direct him to a solution to *that* problem – not some other. Second, we don't think that there is a need for medication. Indeed, at times, medication might even impede progress. But Dr. Burns isn't interested in medication either, since he doesn't practice medicine. There are two basic ways people define depression: 1) in a folksy way – as when someone complains, "I'm down," or "I'm blue"; 2) in a more serious way: when one is "down-and-out." By that I mean, when he has ceased functioning in a large number of areas. Thus, he ceases to meet his responsibilities. Pressures mount. People expect things that are not done. Deadlines aren't met, etc. If a preacher gets behind in his studies and preaches off the cuff, for instance, he might – at length – become "depressed" and quit preaching altogether. He may say, "I just can't go on" ("can't" being a favorite word of depressed people). Or, if a teacher allows the bluebooks to pile up un-graded, week after week, he too may eventually reach a similar point. You see…

Prof. Burns: Ouch! I've never let it go that far, but I've sometimes been on the road!

Greg: So, for instance, when a housewife – for whatever reason – gets "down" (perhaps she's had the flu and been unable to do the chores for a week), as she emerges from bed, she looks at the mess that one husband and two sons have made, and tells herself, "I'm just too weak to do anything about it today." So, she goes back to bed. The next day she feels worse because she is guilty of having failed to put at least a dent in the mess yesterday. So, for another day her "helpful" family members go on piling more on the mess. Then, taking one look at the accumulating disorder, she decides she's not up to dealing with it and again returns to bed. If this continues, before long she will become depressed. If a person is down and feeling bad because of guilt, of course he must repent and deal with his sin. Sometimes, it is more complicated than this, but I'm simply laying out some principles.

Now, how do we help such persons? By sending them back to deal with their neglected responsibilities *no matter how they feel.* As the housewife's mess gets lower, her spirits get higher, just as when the pile got higher, her spirits lowered. Depression leads to quitting, giving up. The more one neglects, the worse he feels; the worse he feels, the more he neglects until, at last, he stops functioning altogether. The problem is this: he follows his feelings rather than his responsibilities.

The dynamic is clear from Paul's letters. He says, "We are afflicted in all sorts of ways (read II Corinthians 6:4–10; 11:23ff. for details), but not crushed; perplexed, but not given to despair" (II Corinthians 4:8). How is it that Paul didn't despair, that he wasn't depressed, and didn't give up when he had to endure so much? He never copped out. He continued to preach throughout it all. Nothing stopped him. When the Jews stoned him and left him for dead at Lystra, I'm sure he didn't *feel* like going on. But he did. When beaten and shipwrecked, he must have *felt* like quitting. But he didn't. Problems like flu, sinful deeds, persecution, whatever, do not *cause* depression. They are but occasions that may lead to it if not dealt with biblically. The Bible refers to such occasions for sinning as "stumbling blocks." It warns about them and also explains how to avoid tripping over them.

But what is it that made Paul go on instead of quitting? He tells us, "Therefore, since we have this service to perform as the result of mercy, we don't give up" (II Corinthians 4:1). One thing motivated him: gratitude. He was so profoundly thankful for his salvation and the ministry God gave him that he would not stop ministering until God called a halt to his ministry! The same is true of depressed persons: when they are helped to become grateful to God for what He has done, they can – and will – persevere, no matter how they feel. A person avoids depression by fulfilling his responsibilities even when he doesn't feel like it, and he emerges from depression when, in spite of his feelings, he starts assuming neglected responsibilities once more – *no matter how he feels*. That last phrase is the key. We have had many people get out of depression in a week or two. It doesn't take months or years, or gobs of medicine to do the job. Incidentally, we neither prescribe nor de-prescribe medicine. That's not our task, and it isn't correct for us to do so. Many of our counselees – on their own, or under the direction of a physician – drop medications altogether.

Bob: Well, that's an interesting scenario that you've presented. But, when you say that you point a counselee to what God has done for him, so that in gratitude he will pick up on his responsibilities once more – what if the counselee isn't a Christian?

Greg: Great question, Bob. Jane, I see that you're just dying to answer. Go ahead.

Jane: Thanks. Bob, it's no problem. They don't counsel non-Christians. Remember the lecture outline that Phil duplicated and handed out to everyone? I think there's a section on it explaining that. They "precounsel" unbelievers – i.e., evangelize them.

Prof. Burns: But what of unbelievers? Don't nouthetic counselors care about them?

Greg: Of course we do. Actually, we care so much that we don't want to give them false assurance. If we were to help them make certain unbiblical life changes that would give them hope that they are now pleasing to God, we would fail them. You see, the unbeliever "cannot please God" (Romans 8:8). It isn't our business to move unbelievers from one lifestyle that displeases God to another that displeases him. To move an unbeliever to a more comfortable lifestyle doesn't do him any eternal good, and whatever solutions he thinks he has arrived at are not God's. So, in the long run, we have harmed rather than helped him. We evangelize him. If he believes, we counsel him. If not, we keep evangelizing until he believes or leaves – as in all evangelism.

Prof. Burns: Sounds a bit cold to me.

Phil: May I answer that one?

Greg: Sure.

Phil: Well, you see…

Milt: Pardon me. I just looked at my watch and I have to be leaving. I'm not running out. Can we meet again?

Greg: OK by me. How about the rest of you? [Phil prays. All agree and set a time one week from today, and leave, not without a piece or two of cold pizza!]

CHAPTER TWELVE

[In the evening, one week later, the group returns. No one is missing. Greg, as host, opens the discussion after passing out refreshments.]

Greg: It's so good to see you all again. Shall we start where we left off – about how, knowingly, we don't counsel unbelievers?

Prof. Burns: No. After thinking things through and talking further with Phil, I can see that, from your perspective, you probably *ought* to consider it harmful to a non-Christian to allow him to gain a false assurance that he is right with God when he isn't. Phil also told me a bit about the fact that not counseling doesn't mean not helping – as some wrongly have supposed. He put it succinctly: You will do good to unbelievers, but not allow them to think that they are doing good by outwardly behaving like Christians. I agree that hypocrisy isn't good in God's sight. I must say, from my own experience, I've wondered from time to time how much good psychology has to offer unbelievers by doing little more than making them more successful temporally or helping them feel better. Not that I buy this view, you understand, but I can see your point, which makes sense given your presuppositions.

Greg: Well, that's pretty much how we see it. It's sad to "help" someone with what, in the end, isn't true help at all. Sort of like recommending smoking in order to lose weight. You may follow that advice and lose weight, but end up with lung cancer! If that matter's no longer on the table, what would you like to consider now?

Jane: In class this week, we've been trying to compare various psychologies with nouthetic counseling. So far, we've looked at Rogers and Freud.

Greg: And what did you conclude?

Phil: Let me take up Rogers – if that's agreeable to the rest of you – and I think that Brian would like to say something about Freud. Then we'd appreciate *your* comments. OK?

Greg: Sounds good to me. But, before you do, may I make one important observation?

Phil: Of course.

Greg: We consider Rogers, Freud, and all other psychiatrists and psychologists who counsel, theologians – nothing more, nothing less. You should understand this fact, if we're going to engage in such a discussion. So inevitably, counseling – as we see it – comes down to a discussion of theology.

Prof. Burns: What? You're full of surprises! *That's* a new one on me. Freud, Rogers – theologians? So far as I know, none of them did theology. And I don't see how they could be called theologians. How can you say this? I'm not a theologian; I can assure you of that!

Greg: I said theologians, not good ones! [some laughter] Nor were most of them aware of the fact that they were teaching and practicing theology. Each taught a doctrine of man upon which he based his system. And, consequently, when consistent, he dealt with man on the basis of that doctrine. Rogers, for instance believed, as he said, that, at the core of his being man is essentially good. He thought, as a result, that man comes into the world prepackaged (my terminology) with the proper answers to his problems. He needs no outside assistance. Indeed, a doctrine of dependence upon divine revelation is fatal to true help. The difficulty, he taught, is that people depend on others – authorities, the Bible, grandmother – for help, instead of trusting themselves. He wanted to redirect counselees toward their own inner solutions. That's why he developed his reflective methodology. So, our difficulty with Rogers is that, according to his theology, the Bible, preaching, the church – even God – are all harmful, because they propose solutions from without. And his fundamental concept, that man is essentially good, is contrary to Scripture as well. His theological views sharply negate the need for a Savior and even for counseling itself. Once, in addressing a group of teachers, he went so far as to say that teaching is impossible. Why? Because it is inculcating data from without. On the basis of Rogerian theology, man is his own savior, who discovers truth within.

Phil: I can see now that I don't need to take up Rogers after hearing that. Obviously, attempts at integration would be hopeless. No wonder you say Rogerianism is not for Christians!

Brian: Frankly this view of psychologists as poor theologians fascinates me And rather than me talking about Freud, Pastor Greg, I'd like to hear you explain something about *his* theology. It seems almost humorous to think of Freud as a theologian!

Greg: It does, doesn't it! I will, if that's agreeable to all. [Affirmations both verbal and non-verbal are given.]

Prof. Burns: All of this sounds goofy – if you allow me the word. But this whole approach is so different from anything I've ever heard, I've got to hear you out. Please go on.

Greg: Very well, then. Freud's theology is equally abhorrent to Christians who recognize what it is. According to him, man is not responsible for what he does. People, he thought, are driven by a mass of irrational forces in the unconscious. These have been socialized into him over the years. They constitute the bulk of the iceberg beneath the water [his metaphor]. The conscious, rational side of man is the peak of the iceberg protruding above. Man uses this meager bit of rationality to rationalize his otherwise irrational drives. That's why, no matter what a counselee tells his counselor, the latter always looks for a different explanation. Since others have made him into what he now is, through socializing their views into his unconscious, he isn't responsible for what he does. So, the only help to be offered is to pry into his past to discover what slugs lie beneath every flat stone you can upturn in order to

71

squash them. Freudian theology, it turns out, proposes an attack upon a person's conscience. Now, think of this theology in contrast to Christianity. Contrary to Freud, God *does* hold man responsible for what he does: He clearly tells us that we all must die and that, thereafter, He will bring us into "judgment" (Hebrews 9:27). That sounds to me like God will hold men accountable for what they do. Agreed? Many problems in society today come from the permeating influence of Freud's doctrine of human non-responsibility. Moreover, God deals with man as a rational creature. For instance, He says, "Come now, let us reason together" (Isaiah 1:18). And we are commanded to give a reasoned defense (*apologia*) of the faith that is within us (I Peter 3:15). It's even foolish for one Freudian psychiatrist to accept at face value anything that another Freudian psychiatrist says. The old cartoon says it all. Two of them pass by one another and say "Hello." Three paces beyond, each stops and says, "I wonder what he meant by that." [A few snickers and one hearty guffaw!]

Dawn: This is all so different from anything I've ever heard before.

Bob: Yeah. Think of it – psychologists as theologians!

Prof. Burns: I'm quite surprised at what you're saying. I admit, I didn't expect anything like this!

Greg: Well, there's no reason to think that God's way of looking at things is the same as that of man's. God is the God of surprises. Sometime, you might want to look up Isaiah 55:8 to see why God's ways are surprising. [several jot down the reference in their notes]

Phil: [Obviously pressing for more.] What about Skinner's theology?

Greg: That's an easy one. He believed that man is only an animal and must be controlled the same way you control animals – by reward and aversive control (punishment – though he refused to admit it). What's wrong with that? Just this: man is far more than an animal. He is a special creation, made in the image and likeness of God, and must be treated as such.

Phil: One reason I asked is because some have called nouthetic counseling a form of behaviorism.

Greg: They do that because we speak plainly about behavior (as if all systems didn't!) However, we talk openly about man's sinful behavior and how he can change and behave righteously. We talk about behavior because, thousands of years before Wundt or Skinner, God talked about behavior. All views of controlling behavior are not the same. We teach that God, the Spirit, dwelling within, is the One Who changes behavior for good. He persuades us to live biblically by changing our hearts' desires (cf. Philippians 2:13), thus motivating us to do God's will, and by empowering us when we attempt it. That's our type of "behaviorism," if you will! The Holy spirit was poured into the believer's heart for the express purpose of enabling him to love God and his neighbor (cf. Romans 5:5).

Phil: Let me write those verses down so I can study them later [Greg references them again, adds I Peter 1:17–19, and Phil and the others write them down in their notes.]

Milt: It sounds far-fetched, doesn't it? Imagine trying to fit the Holy Spirit into psychological counseling!

Greg: Let me also clarify one other thing – it's the understanding that the Bible gives us of love. Love isn't a feeling first and foremost. Listen to the following biblical citations about love and tell me what is common to them: "He loved me and gave Himself for me"; "Husbands love your wives as Christ loved the church and gave Himself for her"; "God so loved the world that He gave His only begotten Son." You can finish it.

Dawn: I've got it – giving!

Greg: As the Brits say, "Spot on!" Love isn't feeling good because one is *getting* something for *himself* ("She must meet my needs!"), but it's *giving* to another ("I must meet her needs"). That's why you can "love your enemies," as Christ directed. You can always do good – even to an enemy – by "giving" him whatever it is that he needs – whether you feel like it or not.

Milt: I can hardly believe what I'm hearing. I've been told that nouthetic counselors are hard customers with little or no compassion or love at all. What a difference this is from that appraisal. But is it more than Christianity you're offering after all?

Greg: No. Jesus Christ has the answers to men's problems. That's basic Christianity. Nouthetic counseling is but one aspect of applied Christianity. Or, better still, perhaps, it's best described as Christian doctrine applied to Christian living gone wrong. You can hardly believe anything that you hear about nouthetic counseling from others. There's a lot of mis-information out there. Some is deliberate. Most, I want to think, is not. We don't hit people over the head with a Bible. We don't think that every difficulty one has is the result of his sin (though all difficulties in life ultimately come from Adam's sin). We gather data – we don't think that one answer fits all. The most extensive discussion of data gathering I know is found in Adams' *Christian Counselor's Manual*. We believe in genuine counseling, not in some quick fix. Much of the misinformation comes from people who haven't read nou-thetic counseling materials, but have accepted and passed on gossip about it. Phil, you did explain to the group why we aren't eclectic borrowers of others' methods, didn't you?

Phil: I did. I pointed out the difference between means and methods, making it clear that all, being human beings, must use the same means (speech, listening, etc.), but that their methods differ because methods are means committed to achieving the ends of systems.

Prof. Burns: Getting back to us psychologists as theologians, do you think we also have "doctrines" of God, the church, the future, etc.?

Greg: Absolutely. Not necessarily articulated as such. And, probably accepted uncritically in most cases. No psychological system takes God into account for what He is. Otherwise, they'd accept His description of human problems, and they'd use His methods designed to reach His ends. Their ultimate end, for instance, would not be the relief of counselees but new attitudes and behavior that glorify God. No system but a biblical one has this doctrine of God's supremacy and honor in all things as its goal. Other systems don't call counselees to repentance when appropriate, or enforce church discipline, and so forth. As to the doctrine of the church, much could be said, but let me mention just one thing. If psychologists believed that God's Word had the answers, they'd be operating under the authority and aegis of the church – with all the resources that it provides. As to a doctrine of the future – well, we have already mentioned the importance of helping potential counselees come to Christ as Savior rather than seek some temporal solution to their problems. We help counselees knowingly work toward eternal goals rather than mere temporal ones. We teach that attitudes and behaviors have eternal consequences – and that fact has strong influence upon human motivation. Of course, these few words about how biblical doctrines are central to counseling only lightly *touch* the subjects, you understand. I give entire lectures about each and courses on some.

Prof. Burns: Well, I can say one thing for you people – you have certainly thought through a lot more than I realized, and some of your observations are tantalizing. But, for the most part, what you've been saying sounds naive – simplistic – if you allow me to say so without taking offense.

Greg: None taken. Simple, yes; simplistic, no. Truth simplifies; error complicates. God's ways are actually profound. But their expression need not be complex. Much by others that *sounds* sophisticated is nothing more than ordinary concepts (some of which are vapid) plastered over with jargon. Psychology and psychiatry are especially prone to use it. The word "schizophrenia" is a good example.

Prof. Burns: But what you said about depression can't be all that simple. Many people take years of therapy to come out of depression. Only medicine seems to help others.

Greg: Evidently, then, psychotherapeutic treatment has little to offer them. So, the next time you counsel a depressed person, why not give our "simple" method a try?

Prof. Burns: Uh…I don't do counseling. I just teach it.

Greg: I see. Did you ever counsel?

Prof. Burns: Not exactly. We dabbled with it in grad school; observed it through one-way mirrors…

Greg: Did you ever observe depressed persons helped out of their depressive states?

Prof. Burns: I guess I never had the opportunity to observe a case of depression.

Greg: It must make it hard to teach counseling when you've barely done it.

Prof. Burns: Uh…well, no. I've studied the literature thoroughly and, basically, what I do is teach and evaluate theories.

Greg: I see…

Milt: Pastor Greg, you mentioned schizophrenia. Surely, that's a complex subject. And a disorder that you probably don't handle – right?

Greg: It's only complex for one reason: the term is meaningless. At one time it might have had a narrower, more specific referent, but today it is used as a label for all sorts of bizarre behaviors. I agree with Karl Menninger who said, "Schizophrenia? To me, that's just a nice Greek word." Menninger, at the time, was considered the dean of American psychiatrists.

He understood that the word was a catch-all. Adams once wrote a chapter on schizophrenia in a book entitled, *The Construction of Madness* (edited by Peter Megaro and published by the University of Maine at Orono). Each chapter was penned by a different person – the rest of whom were psychiatrically oriented. It turned out that no two authors agreed about what schizophrenia is, let alone about how to treat it. The reason, of course, is that the word is used to label all sorts of bizarre behavior – regardless of etiology. It is like calling someone with a red nose a rummy. A red nose may come from all sorts of widely-varying causes: growing a pimple on it, having one's wife punch him in it, falling asleep under the sun lamp – you name it! That means each case must be examined separately. The word is virtually useless. In some instances, sleep deprivation may cause hallucinations, while in others (as in David's case when fleeing for his life to the Philistines) you may be dealing with someone who is malingering. Those are but a couple of many other possibilities. Some cases have an organic base, and must be treated medically. Many others are not organic. They are cases where people are dealing badly with life's many problems. We do deal with the latter.

Brian: My brain's reeling! You're causing me to have a paradigm shift! Former thoughts and structures are crumbling and new ones have been appearing.

Greg: Of course. That's what God calls – in simple language – "repentance." The Greek word *metanoia* refers to a radical change of mind. You see, you're discovering that it's impossible to successfully hold to God's ways and man's ways at the same time. The reason is that all other systems are in competition with His. And – as the Old Testament vividly demonstrates – God disapproves of His competition! Tell me this: do other systems aim at producing love, peace, joy, patience in their counselees?

Brian: Most do, I'm certain.

Greg: Well, God calls these characteristics the "fruit of the Spirit" (Galatians 5:22ff). That is to say, they are the result of the Holy Spirit's work in the believer. If those who hold to other systems also claim they can produce peace, joy, etc., *apart from* or in *some other way than* by the Spirit's work, there can be nothing less than a systems clash. Obviously, all integration, therefore, is not only a pipe dream but, also, an attack on the truth of God's Word. The claims of late-coming psychotherapists (millennia after the Scriptures were written) are but an attempt to overthrow the biblical system with ones of their own. This may not be the conscious aim of all of their advocates, but it is surely the aim of the one who has always tried to get man to doubt and deny God's Word.

Brian: Whoosh! There goes another piece of my paradigm!

Dawn: There are numerous groups out there purporting to do biblical counseling. One is called "Healing of Memories." Do you subscribe to that?

Greg: As a matter of fact, no. There are three fundamental reasons for rejecting the system:

1. Memories don't get sick! [snickers].

2. The Bible knows nothing of it.

3. The view is a substitute for something that the Bible does teach.

The system is an attempt to find an easier way out of bad relationships with others than the biblical way. God's way is through confession, forgiveness and reconciliation. Memory-healing avoids the usual immediate unpleasantness that is involved in doing as God requires, but in the long run may actually lead to more unpleasantness. Actually, it's a selfish system because it ignores the person who did the wrong and makes no effort to bring him to repentance. This and a number of other false views of forgiveness are mentioned in Adams' book on the subject.

Dawn: What's the name of that book?

Greg: *From Forgiven to Forgiving*. It's available from Timeless Texts.

Milt: Do you have to confront people about every little wrong?

Greg: Absolutely not. God says in Proverbs 10:12, "Love covers all sorts of transgressions." If husbands and wives had to sit down and deal with every slight or rub, they'd be doing it all day long – and, in some cases, nothing else! It's the matters that come between people that must be dealt with that way (see Matthew 18:15, where it speaks of "winning" one's brother). It's those situations in which one is so estranged that he must be won back into friendship and fellowship.

Prof. Burns: Actually, I'm ready to call it an evening. I appreciate the invitation and the temper of the discussion. I have also been enlightened about nouthetic counseling.

Greg: Shall we set another date to gather for more discussion next week? [Assent and prayer.]

CHAPTER THIRTEEN

Phil: Prof's not coming! [Phil's first words as the group assembled in Greg's study.]

Greg: Oh? Some problem?

Phil: He says there's only one week left in this semester, and he has too many tests to grade. "You wouldn't want me to get depressed, would you," were his very words. Then, he won't be available later on since he's going off on vacation during his sabbatical leave next semester. He asked me to explain.

Dawn: We're all here except Milt. He asked me to take notes for him and he said that he'd be present next time. He didn't offer a reason for missing tonight; he asked me to tell you that it was unavoidable.

Greg: Well, that's good of him. I'm sorry that we won't have his input, but we'll look forward to seeing him next time. That is, if the rest of you want to continue weekly meetings until you've heard enough.

Jane: We've talked a lot among ourselves and we would like to pursue matters as far as seems profitable. So, we'll be quite happy to continue.

Greg: Fine. How did the rest of your oral reports go?

Brian: Not as well as Phil's, but he had a lot of help. I think we all did well enough, however. Pastor, there's something I've been dying to ask you, but we never got around to it. You know, we shouldn't have to put up with psychology courses of this sort in a Christian institution, should we? And – think – I came here to major in psychology because I wanted to help people. I was told that's *how* to help people. Now, I've discovered that there's no real help in psychology – a conclusion that I've been coming to all semester – so, like Phil, I've dropped my psych major. Like him, I'm also considering the pastorate. But, tell me, if you can, what's wrong with Christian schools, and how did they get this way? Why do they want to have psych majors anyway? And what can we do about the situation?

Greg: Well, I'm glad to hear that you've seen the light about psychology. Just be sure that the ministry is where you ought to serve Christ. If there's any way I can help you make your decision – let me know. Now, about Christian institutions: not everything is wrong about them; there is much that's good. But about the teaching of counseling psychology (I'd include sociology along with it), that's another matter. This is a discipline that is opposed to Christian thought and practice. It has no place in a Christian organization, let alone a Christian school. How did we get into such a mess? Let me hazard a guess or two, and see what you think.

First, there's the fundamental problem of accreditation. For some reason – prestige, or whatever – Christian schools think that they must have it, and great is the joy when they achieve it! Frankly, I believe that it's hurt more than helped them. When you go for accreditation, you must agree to someone else's standards – those set by non-Christians. That's a bad beginning. You must also teach certain subjects, psychology being one of them. A further requirement is a heavily-degreed faculty. So, schools seek the teacher with the Ph.D. rather than the person who has the goods (with or without some higher degree behind his name). Occasionally, you can find both in one person, and happy is the school that does! But more often than not, the teacher with the degree is chosen over the dedicated and biblically knowledgeable one without a degree.

Then, along with accreditation and degrees goes the matter of tenure. Mediocre people – or those who have become satisfied to teach the same course that they have taught for the last five years without changes or improvement – are kept on the faculty because, once tenured, it's very difficult to remove them. Also, along with this is the matter of "academic freedom" guaranteed by accreditation. This can mean teaching "anything that I want," even though it may not agree with good biblical doctrine. Indeed, in order to win students and influence people, doctrinal standards of schools are pared down to the bare minimum.

Most teachers are not good exegetes or theologians. In addition to a solid background in their area of teaching (most of which they may have learned at non-Christian institutions), they need a thorough knowledge of the Bible. Instead, in most cases, I'm afraid, their understanding of the faith is either weak or distorted. And finding those who know how to teach their subjects biblically (that's the higher degree that Christian teachers really need!) is about as difficult as finding a lost work of Shakespeare! I could say much more, but how's that for starters?

Brian: Exactly the sort of thing that I wanted you to cover, and it makes sense. What you're saying – though you didn't actually say it – is that we need to start over again. This time, we should ignore accreditation and all that flows out of it, establish biblical standards, and go our own way as Christians.

Greg: Probably so, because once the accreditation process is in place, it's nearly impossible to eliminate it. But you're talking about a mammoth task, and there may be few that will agree to it. For most, it's just easier to let things go on as they have in the past.

Bob: But without accreditation, does a degree from a school mean much?

Greg: It depends. That can be a problem for undergrads who want to go on for grad studies. But there are schools that, by the quality of their product, become self-accrediting. I understand that for years Harvard was not accredited. But, sure, if you want to make radical changes, you have to be willing to take your lumps. I'd like to see some worthy Christian institutions begun that would give first and full consideration to these matters. In the meantime, I suppose, we might as well go to Babylonian U, as Daniel did. If we are careful not to be taken in by error when doing so, we ought to grow stronger for having bucked whatever error the Babylonians teach. That's one way – awkward and inadequate as it may be – to grow stronger in faith and the knowledge of God's Word. But that takes courage and understanding of what you're getting into. For most, a Christian institution – with all of its faults – is best. The greatest danger in attending a Christian school rather than Babylonian U, however, is deceiving yourself into believing that what you are getting is biblical, whether it is or not. Many uncritically accept what they are taught: "If it sounds Christian, it must be. After all, professor Joe Smow, who says so, is a Christian." It's easier to become complacent in a Christian context than in a non-Christian one. Churches should arm their students-to-be with an understanding of biblical presuppositions, teach them to be discerning, and train them to use their Bibles effectively. But, again, how many do so? And, how many parents and children are willing to learn?

Jane: Do all nouthetic counselors hold these views about academia?

Greg: I'm afraid not. I could be wrong, and they could be right, but I don't think so. Shall we leave this subject and go on to discuss some nouthetic counseling matters? It's taken us too far afield from nouthetic counseling.

Brian: Where can a person get an education in nouthetic counseling?

Greg: There are a few colleges and seminaries that offer such studies. But for those who have already graduated, or are not called to pastoral counseling work, I recommend the distance learning program offered by the Institute for Nouthetic Studies. You can access their web site at www.Nouthetic.Org. They will gladly send you a catalog.

Dawn: I'm concerned about the process of change that takes place in nouthetic counseling. You've indicated that it doesn't take months and months, or even years, to deal with most problems, as some others do. How is it that nouthetic counselors are able to bring about such rapid change in counselees?

Greg: Great question. There are several reasons. First, as you know, we counsel Christians. These are people with potential for life changes: they have the Spirit at work within, enabling them to understand the Bible and to do what God requires. So, we don't have to work alone. I said some things about that in the lecture outline that I gave out. You might want to peruse it again. In addition, we don't expect change to take place during the counseling hour. Unlike other systems, we don't consider this the magic hour when everything important takes place. Our counselors are not magicians who sprinkle whiffle dust on their counselees to carry them throughout the week until they can see them again in a week. Our counseling sessions are more of a teaching, decision-making, and commitment time. Matters are discussed and counselees make commitments to do biblical things during the week to come. They are then turned loose with God as their Partner to live differently during that week, and to report on progress at the next session. So, instead of trying to change people in a fifty-minute period once a week, we expect change to go on all week long. Change happens in the milieu in which the problems arose, not in an artificial setting like a counselor's office. There is a good bit of material concerning this in Adams' *Manual*.

Jane: But what if your counselee's caught in some problem from which he just can't seem to extricate himself – something like homosexuality or drunkenness?

Greg: We call those problems life-dominating sins. They bring about sin-dominated lifestyles. The key to understanding and dealing with these kinds of problems is found in Ephesians 5:18, where Paul speaks about drunkenness. There he commands the drunkard to be "filled with the Spirit" (instead of spirits!). Now, that phrase must be understood. Don't think of filling your car's gas tank. Rather, picture a large auditorium full of empty seats. As the crowd comes in, seats are taken until, at last, the auditorium is "full" to capacity. Every chair is occupied. And now, switch to a different metaphor. Look at the slices of that pizza you've been eating. Think of each slice as an aspect of life: physical life, social life, work or school life, family life, church life, and so forth. It doesn't matter how many slices you have, so long as you take in the whole pizza. God isn't confined to any one slice; He's over the whole of one's life. Now, when the bottle gets hold of someone, it permeates ("fills") his life. It gets into every slice of life, sits on every chair in the room. It dominates him so that everything is not only affected by it, but controlled by it. Following repentance, whenever needed, we must help him to replace the sin in each slice with its biblical alternative – Spirit produced "fruit." Each area must be captured and restructured for Christ.

Jane: I can see now why so many Christian alcohol treatment programs fail. Their focus is too narrow.

Greg: Exactly. All too often they are just "Christianized" versions of AA.

Jane: Their whole life needs to be changed by the Holy Spirit from the inside out.

Greg: Well, what shall we discuss next?

Dawn: I'd also like to know something about the place of women in nouthetic counseling. I don't want to violate I Timothy 2 where women are forbidden to engage in doing the two works of an elder, teaching and ruling. So, what, if anything, can I do?

Greg: I think this is important...

Phil: May I make a suggestion here?

Dawn: Sure.

Phil: Well, I had a great woman counselor who helped me a lot – my mother!

Greg: Of course, as you are suggesting, women are to counsel children – but also other women.

Phil: That's two-thirds of the job!

Greg: Granted. All unordained Christians – men or women – are commanded to counsel informally. Formal counseling is restricted to elders as a part of the task to which they were ordained. But every believer should be prepared to counsel informally. When you have the time, study the meaning of Galatians 6:1 and Colossians 3:16. Formal counseling has the spiritual authority mentioned in Hebrews 13:17. Neither unordained women nor men are to counsel that way. So, fundamentally, the issue is ordination, not gender. Dawn, as a believer who will need to be able to help others from time to time, you should equip yourself to do all sorts of informal counseling.

Dawn: I appreciate the explanation.

Brian: I have another topic.

Greg: Yes?

Brian: Doesn't *too* much counseling go on in the church?

Greg: Yes, definitely. In one sense, counseling isn't all that important. It's only remedial. Counseling is an emergency measure that is taken when the flow of sanctification (Christian growth) becomes plugged up. The counselor is, in effect, a plumber (or a can of Drano, if you will!). If the work of pastoral care were done as it ought to be done, there would be less need for counseling.

Bob: Could it be that good preaching would make counseling unnecessary?

Greg: No, everything can't be done through preaching. In Acts 20:31, we read that Paul counseled day and night for the three years that he pastored at Ephesus. If the apostle Paul couldn't pull it off by preaching alone, neither can we do so today! When you get time, you might also study Acts 20:20.

That harmful old phrase, "The Primacy of Preaching," which has given many preachers an excuse for not doing counseling, isn't biblical. Preaching is absolutely critical, but it isn't prime. We should give primacy to the "ministry of the Word" (Acts 6) in all of its forms. Many congregations could also lessen the need for counseling by practicing good care and discipline of their members. Too many troubled Christians are allowed to fall through the cracks. Many problems, nipped in the bud, would not progress to the point where counseling is necessary. Proper care and discipline could forestall the need for *most* counseling, I think. The reason counseling has assumed such an important place in the church today is the poor quality of elder care. There are wounded, bleeding Christians lying all over the battlefield unattended, that can't fight the Lord's battles because of their own need for help. No wonder the church is so weak!

Phil: Well, this has all been enlightening again, as always. How about telling us something about love and marriage. So many marriages are falling apart.

Greg: What do you want to know?

Phil: Oh…something about the basics.

Greg: OK. But this isn't the time or place to do premarital counseling! Let me begin by reminding you that love isn't getting, but giving. To base a marriage on love, when it is conceived of as a feeling, is a sad mistake that many make. If you read the marriage ceremony that most pastors use, it *enjoins* love on the couple being married. Love is viewed as an *obligation* of marriage ("I promise to love, honor…"), not as a *ground* for marriage. One ought to marry another in order to devote his life to blessing that person whom he marries in the Lord. He ought not ask, "What can I get out of marriage," but rather, "How can I give of myself to my husband or wife?" Good communication also is essential to good marriages. In my book – if I haven't given you each a copy of it, you're welcome to have one; they're on that shelf over there – you will find a lot about its importance. No need to discuss it here, since you can all read! Was there anything specific that you had in mind?

Phil: Well...no. I suppose those are the basic matters.

Jane: I guess it isn't any secret to those who are here (except for you, Pastor Greg) that Phil and I have been contemplating marriage. That's – I hope – why he asked about it!

Phil: [reddening in the face] uh...yeah, I guess that's what I had in mind.

Greg: That's just great! I suspected as much. Please let me know when you finalize your thinking. Perhaps I would have more to say then. There are many concepts common to all premarital nouthetic counseling sessions, but there are also quite a number of things that must be individualized as well. No two people come to marriage with exactly the same backgrounds. To ask everyone to jump through the same hoops is foolish. But, of course, your own pastor, back in your home town will do premarital counseling and marry you.

Phil: Uh...you see, we were wondering if you...

Jane: He means that if (or "when") we are about to get married, we'd like you to both precounsel and marry us.

Greg: It's quite kind of you to ask, but I wouldn't want to jeopardize your relationship with your own pastor, Jane. You'd have to square it with him first of all.

Phil: Well, we were both also thinking of joining your church and living in this community. After all, there's a good seminary nearby.

Greg: Now, that's a separate question that we should address separately. I don't believe in sheep-stealing, so we'd have to talk about your reasons for the move you're contemplating. And, probably, we'd have to contact your churches about it. I think that we ought to schedule a separate meeting between the three of us if you make up your mind to marry. I'm not suggesting that the group break up, but simply that I meet separately with Phil and Jane as well. Seems like we've reached a natural stopping point. Is next week, the same time okay for the group? [Nods, yes.] Good. Let's pray. [They do and head for the doorway; Phil and Jane, hand in hand.] Jane, Phil, could I speak with you for a moment? [They stop and listen.] Phil, do you and Jane want to get together soon? Say, the day after the group meets, next week – at 4PM?

Jane & Phil: Agreed.

Greg: [Looking out the window.] The rest are waiting for you. [They hurry out. Greg says to himself:] Well, this is getting interesting! I wonder how it all will turn out.

CHAPTER FOURTEEN

[It's next week. The group arrives on time.]

Greg: Good to see everyone. Milt, we missed you last week.

Milt: Sorry about that, but I had to attend a family gathering.

Greg: No need for explanations. I just wanted you to know that you were missed.

Milt: Well, Dawn filled me in on the discussion. Her notes are always so complete that I think that I'm probably up to speed with the rest of you. At any rate, don't let me hold you back.

Greg: Good. Now, what do you want to learn about nouthetic counseling this week?

Bob: In his report, Phil mentioned the three Cs of nouthetic counseling – Concern, Confrontation, Change. I'd like to hear more about what this change is like and how it comes about through counseling.

Greg: An excellent question! I see you've got enough Bibles among you for all to look at one, so let's turn to II Timothy 3:14–17. [pause, while everyone locates the passage]. I guess we all have it, so let me read it to you, as you follow along [he reads]. In these verses we find God's pattern for change. Indeed, Bob, here you'll find answers to both of your questions. Notice, first, Paul is sending his last letter to Timothy to whom he is handing over the baton. He's about to die, and Timothy must continue his ministry in times that the prophet Paul predicts will be very difficult. He describes them in the first 13 verses of the chapter. He assures Timothy that there is only one way to remain faithful even in such times as these. The Word of God will keep him on track. In verse 15, he mentions the Old Testament Scriptures that Timothy had been brought up on. In the previous verse (v. 14) he referred to his own teaching by precept and example. That apostolic teaching, today, is found in the Bible. So, in effect, Paul is saying that the Scriptures of the Old and New Testaments will keep Timothy from wandering. Then, he goes on to remind him about the purpose of his ministry to believers. As he, and every other Christian, was saved by believing the message of the Bible, so too, now that they are saved the Scriptures continue to exert the definitive influence upon their lives. He is to minister to believers from the Bible, which can do four things for a Christian:

1. Set forth God's will for his life ("teach")

2. Expose when he fails to live up to God's will ("convict")

3. Show him how to get out of the messes he gets into ("correct")

4. Tell him how to stay out of trouble in the future ("disciplined training in righteousness")

Using the Bible, as it is read or preached, the Holy Spirit brings about all four aspects of that change. You can read about this in detail in Adams' book, *How to Help People Change*.

Bob: Seems like a logical program.

Greg: Exactly. But there's one more important element in the passage that I might just touch on since we've discussed it before. In verse 17, Paul says (in three different ways) that the Scriptures are sufficient for bringing about this change: nothing more is needed. Anything added would dilute and pervert the pure truth of the Word. Notice – every good task to which a pastor is called – can be fully met by using the Scriptures. God has supplied all that he needs. Since this is so, how dare anyone say that something more is needed when God says otherwise?

Phil: Boy! That's a powerful passage! I don't see how anyone can talk integration or think of borrowing eclectically from others if he understands verse 17!

Jane: But they do.

Greg: Yes, but for different reasons. In some cases, its mere ignorance. They are culpable, but nevertheless, not hostile. In other cases, there is a willful turning of the back on the truth of the verse. Then, of course, there may be many other reasons as well. We can't look into anyone else's heart, remember. But, we don't have to – God does. And that's what counts. Bob, do these verses give you any idea of what change in nouthetic counseling looks like?

Bob: Yes, as I understand you, you are saying that Scripture sets forth God's standards for life, and that when we violate them the Spirit uses the Bible to convict us of our sin. Then, through the Bible, again, He points the way out of trouble and, finally – by means of biblical training – shows us how to stay out of trouble in the future. Right?

Greg: Perfect!

Bob: Moreover, the Bible has all that it takes to bring about that change.

Greg: Exactly!

Milt: And the way out of the messes we get into is through repentance, confession of sin, and forgiveness.

Greg: Correct again. Repentance is changing our minds so dramatically that we change our direction of living. There are two ways in which change takes place: by learning and by repenting. The two may go together – but not necessarily. When one obeys new truth from the Bible as he understands it, he will change apart from repentance. But, in most counseling cases, because there is a lack of obedience on someone's part, there is a need for it. Culpable ignorance of God's Word, through neglect, is inexcusable. Now, what do you want to know in addition? I'm here for you to pump me dry, if you wish! [no immediate response]. Now, let me explain a few things while you think. First, the Christian counselor already knows a lot about his counselee before he enters the room, because Scripture has described him in detail. At points, during counseling, it is useful to reveal God's portrait of him in the Bible. Here, then, is simply another advantage that biblical counselors have over non-biblical ones: they have God's basic description of a human being. Adams tells about a woman saying, "You know me! Who told you about me?" He replied, "God."

For decades, psychologists have been trying (unsuccessfully) to peep into the inner man. But James, for instance, reveals more about man than any non-Christian psychologist ever understood. In an abundance of revelation about man's inner person, he shows us those "works" that will build and integrate one into a complete (*teleios*) person, as well as those "works" that disintegrate and destroy. John points out that Jesus "knew what was in people" (John 2:24). So must a counselor. How did Jesus – as a man – know? According to Isaiah 11:2, He had "the Spirit of understanding" in Him to enable Him to understand people and apply the Scriptures correctly to them. True, He had the Spirit without measure but, as a believer, you have the same Spirit to help you. The saying, "The proper study of mankind is mankind," is patently false. Psychologists who wittingly or unwittingly espoused that dictum have proven it wrong. Their utter failure to understand man is evidence of the fact. The Christian knows that the proper study of man is not the study of man, but the study of the Bible, where he can find what God says about man!

Jane: That's all very helpful. Now, I have a question. Tell me something about crisis counseling.

Greg: An interesting subject. I guess we'd better begin by defining (or at least describing) what we're talking about. After all, for some, unlike Jeremiah writing in Lamentations, their calamities are "new every morning." We're talking about genuine crises. The word "crisis" comes from the Greek *krino* ("to judge, to decide"). It is, therefore, a point of decision, a point at which some (usually significant) judgment must be made. Perhaps the idea is best expressed in our phrase, "turning point." Scripture doesn't use the word "crisis," but such expressions as "day of calamity" (or just "calamity") in Psalm 18:18 or Proverbs 1:26, 27, or "dread," "distress," and "anguish" (as in Proverbs 1:26–27) serve to convey the concept. These words indicate a sudden, overwhelming tragedy or severe distress that comes on a person in such a way that he can't avoid it, but must face it. It is a turning point because true crises usually have strong potential for bringing about change. Crises demand decisions. Those who fail to make them usually end up in worse shape as a result. Now, such an event presents an opportunity to change for the good – or the opposite. It all depends on how the crisis is handled. Crises test and explore the faith and endurance of counselees. They also provide opportunity for significant spiritual growth. Crises tend to rip the seams out of people and dump out their stuffing. You can see more clearly what they are made of. The counselor's task, as you can readily understand, is to help his counselee to use the crisis to make wise, biblical choices and changes that enhance his love for Christ. Crises come in God's providence, for the good of God's people (Romans 8:18). And, if you understand and believe I Corinthians 10:13 that Jane mentioned some time ago, you can see how that can be. God sends no trial into a Christian's life that he cannot handle, if he handles it God's way. If he does so, then he can take advantage of the crisis to grow. True Christians are never completely "done in" by crises. Such passages as Proverbs 11:9; 24:15, 16; 3:25, 26 make this clear. So, counselors

1. Give biblical hope,

2. Show compassion in doing so,

3. Guide counselees through crises God's way,

4. Do so as quickly as possible (and proper),

5. Warn against poor (usually hastily-made) decisions,

6. And assure the counselee of God's blessings in the crisis.

Counselees may be in such a condition that they don't think clearly. While not doing their thinking for them, counselors point to God's ways of thinking. All decisions in a crisis must have, as their uppermost goal, honoring God. Crises provide opportunity to put into practice what one has been taught before. The more good teaching one has, the more likely he will be able to handle the crisis well, if guided correctly through it. "First Aid" in a crisis consists of

Analysis: take the problem apart, and classify it biblically.

Inventory: discover the counselee's manifest spiritual state – attitude, behavior, and resources.

Direction: turn biblical teaching into righteous responses.

Now, I could develop each element of AID into a lecture, or possibly a course, but I think for our purposes I've given you enough of a picture. Can you run with this, Jane?

Jane: [holding up a pile of papers] I think so, but I may get back to you about it when I have time to think through these notes.

Milt: You introduced us to Tom and Harry, who had been in some serious conflict. You were able to help them resolve it. How did you do it?

Greg: Well, I'm not at liberty to talk about cases, so I must answer you generally. Let me outline something of a procedure to follow. Is that OK?

Milt: Sure. I'm listening, and anxious to hear.

Greg: Crisis counseling, that we just talked about, and conflict are often closely related. I suggest that may be why this question occurred to you. Conflict often leads to crises (for example, the law may be brought into it), and crises may lead to conflict (for example, the family of a deceased parent arguing over the will). Most counselees think that situations give rise to conflict. But situations have no power to do so – unless we allow them to. That's because the source of conflict really is within. Study James 4:1–3 on this matter and you'll see what I mean. The Bible focuses on the inner person – his "heart." James calls conflict between believers "war." When Christians fight, Satan is the only winner. Quarreling largely arises out of pride and selfishness – and kindred inner problems. So, that's what the counselor focuses upon. His role as a peacemaker is (according to James 3:18) to bring into counseling "wisdom from above" which, when followed, issues in peace. The counselor often must show how to defeat habits that fight against holy living. Daily crucifixion of one's own desires in favor of God's is essential (Luke 9:28). One person says, "I want it my way," and another says the same. Both must come to the place where they say, "I want it God's way." Much more could be said, but this is the gist of it. Nouthetic counselors have written fully on this subject too. The counselor's task is to pursue peace.

Phil: Sounds like tough stuff.

Greg: You're so right! But joyful work when you see a Tom and Harry walk out as they did.

Jane: Talking about tough stuff, what about people in pain?

Greg: At one time or another everyone experiences pain. The result of the fall was a world in which pain is inevitable. The Westminster Confession of Faith connects sin and misery, seeing misery as a consequence of sin. All pain is felt in the body, but these pains are of various sorts and etiologies. Pain is a major motivating force – for good or evil.

Some suffer more than others. Some pain is the consequence of one's sin. On other occasions, it is inflicted upon one from without as, for instance, in the case of persecution and martyrdom. The choice is not between pain and no pain, but God's concern is how it is viewed and how it is used. Wrong responses to pain include whining, self-pity, violence, anger, denial, and precipitous action. Medical treatments can be both good and bad.

But, what is pain? It is a physiological (bodily) warning that something's wrong. To kill it with pills can be harmful. Warnings ought to be heeded. Bodily causes of pain include sickness, disease, injury and the like. They may involve enlisting the aid of a physician. But there are inner causes of bodily pain that are non-organic (though the pain itself is organic). They may include such things as guilt, fear, worry, consequences of failure, and so on. Something either outside or inside of the body, therefore, may trigger bodily pain.

Helping a counselee develop a proper perspective on pain is of the uppermost importance. He must come to see potential for good in it, since it means that God is at work providentially in his life. And that He is up to something good (Romans 8:28). Part of that perspective is recognizing that pain is temporary, and light in comparison with the glories of pain-free existence in the life to come. It was Paul who let us in on this truth in his letter to the Corinthian church (II Corinthians 4:17).

Jesus, Who suffered more than any of us, left a pattern for us to follow as we walk in His steps (1 Peter 2:21). He did not lash out at His murderers; He went quietly as a sheep led to slaughter.

God's purposes in circumstances may be manifold. Pain may be loving chastisement, it may be punishment, it may be a warning, it may bring about purification, it may be a means for protecting from further injury, and so on. Those who seek to learn from pain may ponder such verses as Psalm 119:67 and 71. In all, there is no excuse for lowering the bar during pain, as some do. Like Job, a Christian must retain his integrity. And, when suffering unjustly, he should refer to I Peter which is a book dedicated to that particular subject. The message of the book may be summed up in the words of the Gospel song, Trust and Obey. Does any of this help, Jane?

Jane: You bet it does. However, I'd like to see this worked out in detail.

Greg: I believe a course in the INS distance learning program would help you. You might give it a try. By the way, I thought of another two elements of conflict resolution: the first is to open up new biblical options for counselees stuck in a conflict; and the second is to show love to enemies. As a last word on the subject, let me refer you to Romans 12:18, which is critical in dealing with believers and unbelievers alike.

Phil: How about calling it a day? We've taken in so much material to think about that we need time to digest it all. [General agreement, prayer, and departure. Greg speaks to Phil as he is leaving.] Is our time with you and Jane still on for tomorrow?

Phil: You bet it is!

Greg: OK. See you then.

CHAPTER FIFTEEN

[Phil and Jane arrive at 4PM on the dot the next day at Greg's study door.]

Greg: Come on in. I was expecting you.

Phil: We've been looking forward to today…

Jane: For sure!

Greg: Well, Phil, if you contemplate becoming the head of a new, decision-making family, perhaps we should begin by you taking the lead. Why don't you pray about this meeting? [Phil does.] A husband is to be the head of his home. You might as well start thinking in terms of taking responsibility for a family. I've noticed that throughout our previous conversations Jane has been anxious to move things ahead. It may well be that you two should talk out this matter between yourselves. I'll leave it to you, and you can let me know what you come up with at our next meeting (presupposing there is one).

Jane: I guess you're right. I do have a tendency to become aggressive in most things that I do.

Greg: Nothing wrong in that, per se, but in a marriage, you must be sure not to usurp your husband's place. Do you understand this and agree?

Jane: I know you're right and I *will* work on it.

Greg: Good. Now, let's hear from Phil. To start things off, why not fill me in on two things: first, tell me at what stage your relationship to one another is at the moment; and second, what, specifically, do you want me to do for you? Those questions should get our discussion under way.

Phil: OK. Here's the situation. If we were to complete this three-year graduate course, we would have two more years to spend at Christian U. We would have our degrees by then. We'd like to get married at the close of this semester, but we're here to get your reading on this as well as on our future education. If I switch to a Bible or Greek major, I've discovered that I'll lose a lot of credits. It would almost be like starting over. So, we want to decide whether to continue our present majors until graduation or to quit. I'm inclined to leave the U and head for Scriptural Presbyterian Seminary across town. I have my undergraduate degree and would be eligible for seminary. Jane has about had it with her psychology courses and wants to quit anyway. She has suggested that after we get married she would go to work while I go to seminary and take a part time job. Perhaps, by the time I get a year or two under my belt, I'll be able to intern at a church, assisting a pastor. What do you think?

Greg: There are a lot of elements in your proposal. Perhaps we should separate them out a bit. First, let's consider quitting grad school. Are you sure this would be the best course? Would it be good stewardship not to finish what you've already begun? Or would it be a waste of time? Have you and Jane weighed the two options carefully?

Jane: We've hardly talked about anything else. I...

Greg: Just a minute Jane. Phil was explaining things, and you broke into our conversation. There's that aggressiveness again! I don't mean to be picky, but if you're going to have a happy and useful marriage, you will have to learn patience.

Jane: Touche.

Greg: Now, please continue, Phil.

Phil: As I was saying, we've worked things out rather fully, and I think that to continue would be a colossal waste of time.

Greg: Jane, do you agree?

Jane: Absolutely!

Greg: OK. Continue, Phil.

Phil: If I continue at the U, but switch majors to Bible or Greek, then I would be taking courses that I will get in seminary anyway. There would be reduplication, and I can't see where that makes much sense. Right?

Greg: There's a lot to what you're saying. But at the end of the present course and seminary you'd have two degrees – an M.Div. and Ph.D. The doctor's degree would be an asset if you ever wanted to teach. Unfortunately, as we have already noted, that's part of the problem with academia: you need the paper on the wall!

Phil: We've considered that, but I have no desire to teach. I've always wanted to work with people – not to teach students. I didn't mean to imply that students aren't people, as it sounded like I was saying. What I mean is that I took a psychology major because I wanted to help people in trouble. But since I've discovered that Christian counseling, done by a pastor, is the way to go, I can't wait to get started. I want to help people make significant changes – those that please God.

Greg: Well, it does sound as if you have thought things through. And you are determined to make the change? How about you, Jane – are you fully on board? You know, it'll mean giving up your graduate work, and putting in a number of years working at a job while Phil studies. Have you given this your full consideration?

Jane: Definitely! I think that I know what it will involve, and I'm willing to go through with it. I'll get my PhT degree, anyway. You know what that is, don't you?

Greg: Sure: "Putting hubby through." It won't be the first time that someone has earned that degree. The main thing about it is that "hubby" will always need to think of it as higher than a Ph.D. in his eyes. And, I'm glad, Phil, that you plan to get at least some part-time work.

Jane: I don't look forward to those three years of work, but if it is the way to get married right away and for Phil to get his seminary degree, I'm more than willing. What I want more than a further degree is to be married and raise a family. He's asked me to marry him, and unless you should convince us that the scheme we've come up with is wrong, that's exactly what I intend to do. If you don't show us why we shouldn't, we plan to leave here today and go buy the engagement ring! Indeed, I'm not only willing to work on my PhT degree, but quite anxious to do it.

Greg: OK. Just checking things out. Now, how about your parents? What do they say to this proposal?

Jane: Mine are quite enthusiastic about it.

Phil: Mine have had some qualms about it – especially, about changing majors. I've had some long talks with them and they've come around. And, they like Jane.

Jane: My parents really like Phil and are happy to do anything that they can to see that we make it through.

Greg: I suppose that you've considered the fact that going to seminary here in town means that you will not be able to live in the communities where your parents live.

Phil: We've been through that with them and they understand. Because our homes are within traveling distance, we will be able to go home now and then on weekends.

Greg: When you do, you should make a point of equally dividing your time between the families. Since they don't live in the same city, your trips will have to alternate. Don't pick favorites – even if your parents try to make you do so.

Phil: That sounds like good advice.

Greg: So, you've pretty well made up your minds, then, I gather. Now, about your church affiliation. Jane, you come from an independent church – right?

Jane: Correct.

Greg: And, Phil, your background is Presbyterian.

Phil: That's right.

Greg: Well, have you thought through what your future affiliation will be? After all, this ought to be a matter of prime concern to both of you. You want to make the decision on the basis of your beliefs. Scripture should determine them, not some expedient or emotional factor. After all, if Phil becomes a Presbyterian minister, Jane, you've got to support and help him to the hilt. What about baptism, for instance? Your church practices immersion and believer's baptism, Jane, doesn't it? When children come along it's too late to make a decision about whether to baptize them or not. You could get into a serious argument that could spread through the congregation. Churches have been split over matters less important.

Jane: I'm studying the whole Presbyterian belief system. I've been thinking about these matters for some time. I've become a Calvinist – no trouble there, I believe in the sovereignty of God and the doctrines of grace. My only hang-up, as you suggested, is over infant baptism.

Phil: We've been working on it. And I appreciate the fact that Jane won't accept anything unless it can be proven from the Scriptures. I wouldn't want her to change her beliefs because of me. She has to be convicted of the matter herself.

Greg: Sounds like you've come a long way doctrinally. But the baptism question is important.

Greg: Well, if you plan to get married at the end of the school year in May or June, you'll have to work this out rather quickly.

Phil: Will you help us?

Greg: If you want me to. But let me ask you this – are you going to get married by Jane's pastor and at her church? That's traditional.

Phil: I think so. My parents and friends live within a couple of hours of her church, so it wouldn't be a hardship for them. I think that this will be best.

Greg: Then, you will want to go talk to her pastor about it, and have him give you pre-marital counseling. You should make it a point to do so rather soon, so that you can make enough weekend trips to consider matters fully. What we've been doing today is not pre-marital counseling, you understand.

Phil: Yeah, I guess so.

Jane: I have already asked him to do it, and he's agreed.

Greg: You really are aggressive, Jane. Not even engaged, and setting up pre-marital counseling? Wow!

Phil: It's OK, Pastor Greg. I agreed before she made the appointment.

Greg: Well, this is a good first visit. From what I've heard, I think that you've got the right idea about things. But before you leave, I'd like to take up one more matter. If you are going to be ordained some day, Phil, you must be a member of a congregation in the denomination in which you will serve, and receive a letter from its elders commending you to presbytery. Phil, you are a member of an apostate presbyterian denomination that has women elders, accepts gay pastors, and, generally, denies biblical truth. I advise you to give serious consideration to leaving it. I think you might find serving in it even more odious than taking grad courses in psychology.

Jane: We've been thinking…[Jane interrupts herself, and then says] There I go again, trying to take the lead. Sorry Phil. You explain our thinking.

Phil: Gladly. Pastor Greg, we both want to unite with your church. What we've seen and heard of the Scriptural Presbyterian Church sounds right to us. I plan to do so right away, and then Jane will do so after our wedding. After all, we'll be living in this community for at least three more years, so we ought to become a part of a local church. If Jane still has some problem with baptism, will she be allowed to join? If you aren't immersed, they won't let you join her church.

Greg: Yes, she will be welcomed into our membership should she wish to join. What we require is a credible profession of faith. We believe that the doors of the church ought to be wide enough to accept any and all who are saved, provided that they have no problems that would cause them to be disciplined out of the church were they a part of it. We don't believe that we can refuse anyone that Jesus Christ has accepted. But we do work hard with all our members to help them understand and accept all of our doctrines. And you two should definitely settle the matter of baptism.

Jane: Good.

Phil: Well, I guess we can go home and digest what we've heard. I hope we can meet again, if we need to.

Greg: Simply let me know and we'll arrange it. I'll look forward to seeing you and the counseling consultation group as agreed upon. Let's pray. [All three pray.]

CHAPTER SIXTEEN

[The group of students from Christian U gathers at Greg's study as planned. Phil and Jane arrive early to show the pastor – and then each student as he enters – Jane's engagement ring. Finally, as the chit-chat dies down, the group seems ready to begin. Brian takes the lead.]

Brian: Well, Pastor, nouthetic counseling certainly does bring people together! [General laughter.] But, seriously, may I ask the first question?

Greg: Of course. But if it has anything to do with marriage – ask Phil, not me!

Brian: I'm just about ready to do the same thing as Phil – no, I don't mean getting engaged – I mean about his plans to enter S. P. Seminary this coming semester. I know you've spoken briefly about the difference between hanging out a shingle on one's own and counseling under the "aegis of the church." Can you enlarge on that point a bit?

Greg: Gladly. As you said, I mentioned this when talking about authoritative counseling versus non-authoritative counseling.

Brian: That's when you made it clear that the distinction isn't between male and female counseling but between ordained and non-ordained persons – whether male or female.

Greg: Exactly. I won't go into that any further, unless you want to, except to state the obvious: Since God ordains people to counsel authoritatively as their task in the church, He considers counseling to be the work of the church. Now, I want to note one great difference between Christians counseling under the authority of the church and those who attempt to do so in some other way. To do the latter is to step out on your own, without His sanction and without the resources that God has provided in His church for helping you counsel. These resources are so numerous that I will only mention a couple here. The counselor, as a minister of the Word, doesn't only counsel but also has opportunity to preach and teach as well. This is a decided advantage over solo counseling, where the church that your counselee attends may teach things that do not coincide with your counsel. Your preaching aids your counseling. Bible studies in certain areas pertaining to the problems of counselees, in addition to and in harmony with counseling, also may add force to the counseling they supplement. Moreover, once he has successfully completed counseling, a minister of the Gospel may pair his counselee with an elder to help mentor him over the weeks to come to assure that he keeps his commitments and doesn't slide back into his former ways.

During counseling, the pastor may encounter areas that require special expertise that he doesn't have. This may include such things as financial advice, homemaking skills, and so forth. In most congregations, there are others to whom the counselor may temporarily hand off his counselee for a session or two to receive such expert assistance. A mother with a problem child may receive better help from a good, successful mother than from a male counselor, and so forth. I'm sure you get the point. The number of possibilities is numberless. A good pastor will call upon his members to serve Christ in this way, and encourage and strengthen them to do so. Consequently, he not only helps counselees, but gives his members outlets for the use of their gifts and knowledge, thereby strengthening and blessing them.

Enough of that; I'm sure you can take it and run with it for yourself from there. Let me now...

Brian: Right! That's a whole new dimension to me. It's fascinating to think of organizing and training a congregation to use their gifts in assisting me as a counselor. Quite a retinue for counseling!

Greg: Isn't it? Remember Tom and Harry? If you took advantage of their offer to talk to them, you'd probably see how you could even benefit in understanding from unordained members of the congregation who are willing to help you.

But let me move to another advantage. Pastoral training at seminary – with all of the flaws of academia – nevertheless provides instruction in the biblical languages and in theology. While not absolutely essential to informal counseling, they are a major asset to formal counseling. A good counselor will want to know all he can about the Scriptures. A person with almost any problem may appear, and the pastor must be ready to address it. A systematic grasp of theology, coupled with an ability to interpret the Scriptures faithfully, provides by far the best training to do so. Of course, there are men who fail to take advantage of their training once they graduate. These men are unfaithful stewards of the blessings that God provided for them – blessings that were intended to be passed on to the members of their flocks. Think of it! Pastors are paid to study and teach the Bible. There is no such needed preparation or continued obligation for the solo counselor who has no such training. He must get what he can helter-skelter as best as possible.[1] Some do as well as could be expected from self-taught efforts, but why begin at such a disadvantage? Moreover, a person who doesn't have the tools from the outset will take a much longer time in acquiring them than the one who has attended a good seminary.

Not only must a minister of God's Word have thought through the wide variety of problems that counselees present, he must have an answer to each of them – or the tools sharp enough to acquire it. In addition, there is the weekly discipline of preaching that, for a faithful preacher, will cause him to regularly learn more of the Bible. This will strengthen his counseling immensely as he is able to bring more and more Scripture, carefully studied, to bear upon counselees' problems. Apart from this regular study, it is easy for one's mind to turn brown, rather than stay green. I have met so-called

---

1. We do teach evening classes in counseling to help informal counselors. These include classes in doctrine and in Bible interpretation.

biblical counselors who think they can counsel everyone from twenty-five verses, or from one book of the Bible. If that were possible, why did God give us so much more?

Brian: Now I see something of the advantages of counseling in the church. I simply hadn't had the understanding of its importance before. Just considering how preaching and counseling serve one another is itself fascinating.

Greg: Yes, and let me say this: as you preach, you will put your finger on problems people have (many of which you will learn about from the counseling room) with the result that members who are struggling with them will come to you for help. Otherwise, they might never have done so, not realizing that God has answers to them. Indeed, some of them would go to the pagan counselor down the street instead! And, in the ministry, a true shepherd gets close to his sheep and can often detect the beginnings of difficulties so as to nip them in the bud, thus forestalling the need for counseling. Counseling and preaching fit snugly together in true ministry (see again the passages in Acts 20 and Colossians 1:28 that I pointed out). So, what God has joined together, let no man put asunder!

Phil: That sounds like a cue for me to speak! [Laughter.]

Greg: Sure! Go ahead!

Phil: I'm so anxious to get into the ministry I can almost taste it! The prospect of doing biblical counseling among the members of a congregation is exciting. But, what about counseling those who come to you who are not a part of your flock? Do you lose some of the advantages that you have just mentioned?

Greg: Good question. Yes and no. Each case will be different in this regard. Some will be members of good churches with faithful pastors who simply haven't been taught the need or methods for counseling. In such cases, we invite the pastor or an elder from the counselee's church to sit in. This does two things: first, it helps us train other pastors in counseling by example; second, it enables us to turn counselees over to the pastor or elder after getting over the major humps so that he may continue sessions to the end. Of course, we instruct them about what must yet be done, we are available for further help when needed, and we often turn a formerly non-counseling pastor into a biblical counselor in the process. I could go on and on about this.

There is one more thing I guess I should say. We rarely counsel a member of another flock that is faithful to the Word without requiring the pastor or an elder to be present. Why should we continue to assume his counseling responsibilities for him? When he sits in, it isn't only the counselee who learns. We want to train him to do his own counseling. If, however, we counsel someone from a congregation that fails to preach the Word faithfully – for instance, a liberal congregation whose teaching will contradict the Bible's – as a part of the counseling we encourage him to leave this church. We do not steal sheep, but when one is sitting week by week under a wolf in shepherd's clothing, that's a different story! Only when there is a radical change in doctrinal beliefs would we encourage Christians to leave a church that isn't liberal.

Milt: Give me an example.

Greg: Sure. Suppose a church teaches that a person can lose his salvation. He comes for counsel saying that he needs to be saved again. First, we must teach him that he is laboring under an unbiblical idea. Then, we deal with his true problem. Having done so, in the process we have taught him to disbelieve what his congregation teaches. Second, we would be unfaithful to return him to a church that would only propagate more of that which we have had to contradict from a scriptural point of view. This would be harmful, not to say unproductive. In such cases, we would try to talk him into joining a congregation that is clearer about such matters. In my first pastorate, I dealt with a teenager who kept telling me that he was saved and lost. Whenever he would turn up, I'd have to ask which he thought he was at that time. He kept

110

going back to the church that taught such things, only to be reinforced with bad doctrine. At that time I didn't know about nouthetic counseling and had not thought through all of the things that I just talked about, or I would have attempted to persuade him to get out from under that teaching. After a while, the kid simply gave up, saying, "I guess I can't keep myself saved," and quit church altogether. It would have been wise to dissuade him from continuing to attend that congregation.

Jane: Well, I guess you've gotten an earful about counseling under the "aegis" of the church – right, Brian?

Brian: Yes, plenty for today, though I'm sure there is much more Pastor Greg could say.

Greg: Right you are!

Brian: Well, sometime, I'd like to meet with you privately to discuss matters about my future a bit more thoroughly. I know we've taken up a lot of time already. Would that be possible?

Greg: I'd be honored to talk further. Would your pastor come with you? Let me know when you are ready. But rather than talking off the cuff, write down all your questions beforehand so that we won't waste your time, and you won't forget anything.

Brian: Will do. Except, my home church is in another state. I doubt that my pastor could come.

Phil: What you just said to Brian is helpful to me too. And it solidifies my intention to become a minister of the Word.

Greg: Excitement is good, but remember, there are lots of difficult times as well as the exciting ones. The ministry is hard work. But it is also very joyous work. There are few things more joyful than knowing that you have helped others appropriate the teaching of Scripture in their lives.

Brian: I have a friend who is in trouble. I don't know all of the details of her problem, but...

Greg: We really don't want to disclose information publicly, anyway. Now, what can we do for her?

Dawn: Well, she was wondering about what to expect from nouthetic counseling, if she decided to come to you for help. She asked me to find out. Can you help me on this?

Greg: I certainly can. Adams has just completed a booklet that is designed for such a purpose., I'll give you, and the rest of the group, a copy – just off the press! It will help her understand what to expect.

Dawn: Thanks. This is exactly what I need. [Copies are distributed. See Appendix B, page 143.]

Greg: Are there other matters you'd like to discuss?

Bob: Could we read through the booklet for a minute and see if there is anything that we might want to ask you? It's short enough for us to read in ten minutes or so.

Greg: Would you all like to do so? Sounds like a good idea to me. [The group agrees and reads.]

Milt: Most of this is pretty straightforward and self-explanatory. But I have one question: Adams mentions the "atmosphere" of nouthetic counseling sessions. Can you enlarge on that?

Greg: Sure. What he's getting at is that a nouthetic counselor wants his counselee *to recognize* that every session is conducted in the presence of God. That means all that is said, every commitment that is made (or not made), and all else that takes place is done before Him. All is done in a context or atmosphere that pleases or displeases Him. Nouthetic counseling is always more than a counselor and counselee conferring.

Milt: Thanks. That surely makes nouthetic counseling different from non-Christian counseling!

Greg: Or even what's done in many so-called Christian counseling sessions! Can you imagine any greater contrast than between the atmosphere that is created in Christian counseling sessions and that created in non-Christian counseling sessions? The nouthetic counselor wants the counselee to see that the principal Person with whom he is dealing isn't the counselor, but God Himself.

Jane: I'd like to hear more about the hope that's mentioned in the booklet. It says that hope leads to perseverance. How is that?

Greg: Well, in counseling, there can be difficult things to do, temporary failures, dry periods, and the like. Counselees (or even counselors) can become discouraged or even give up if they don't have hope. Hope is what carries them through these times to the better ones that lie ahead. Now, don't forget, hope in the Bible is not "hope-so hope." The word means "expectation," and refers to the certainty of God's fulfilling His promises. We always base hope upon the promises that He makes in the Bible. God wants us to hope. Write down Romans 15:4 and 13 in your notes to study sometime. Verse thirteen shows how God wants us to hope, and verse four shows how the Spirit uses the Scriptures to produce hope. In I Thessalonians 1:3, we see how hope is related to endurance. Does that help?

Jane: Yes. But how does the counselor give this hope?

Greg: By opening up the promises of God found in Scripture. Why Jane, your favorite verse, I Corinthians 10:13, is a hope-giving verse if there ever was one!

Phil: I was interested in the concluding section in which the concept of counseling was expanded to more than problem-solving. There, we see that it is inseparably connected to spiritual growth. As a future pastor, I think that I'll find that factor of great significance. It probably is true that lack of spiritual growth is due to the failure of believers to work out difficulties in their lives God's way. And they don't solve growth-stunting problems, in part at least, because either their church doesn't offer true biblical counseling, or if it does, they fail to avail themselves of it. I can see, therefore, Christian counseling as an integral part of one's pastoral ministry. That expansion of my thought makes a large contribution to my vision of the work ahead.

Greg: Well said! [To the group as a whole] What else do you want to know?

Dawn: I think I'm through for the day. I want to get this booklet into the hands of my friend as quickly as possible. I'm heading for her dorm as soon as I leave here.

Brian: Could I briefly bring up one more thing, Dawn?

Dawn: Sure, so long as it's really brief. I know you, Brian – you can go on and on and on...

Brian: OK, OK. I'll make it brief. Pastor Greg, I found on e-bay a copy of a book by Adams called *The Christian Counselor's Casebook*. It's full of slices of counseling cases to be used in role-play. If I bring it in next time, could we look at – or even role play – a couple of cases?

Greg: Would you all like to do so? [General enthusiastic agreement.] Then we will. For now, will you lead us in prayer, Dawn, remembering your friend in need? [Dawn prays, after which the group leaves.]

CHAPTER SEVENTEEN

[The students file into Greg's study door in two groups, chatting as if they were rehearsing something.]

Greg: Hi! What's up?

Jane: You know that this week we were going to discuss cases in the *Casebook*. Well, Brian discovered that we could buy new copies of it directly from Timeless Texts at discount prices. So, we all ordered copies. And we've divided into two groups to practice and role play two cases for you to critique. Is that OK?

Greg: Certainly. It's great! In our Monday evening counseling training program we do role play for ten weeks, and find it very helpful. We use it for three purposes: 1) To teach; 2) To test; 3) To train. We teach biblical principles by acting them out, we test each student's understanding and skill at counseling, and we train him by showing and giving him practice in how to do it. Who will go first, and what case have you chosen?

Phil: Our group will. Our case is # 37, "Imagination?," found on pages 74 and 75. Dawn is our narrator. She will read the case through as it is in the book, and we'll take it from there. Jane and I will play the parts of Janice and Cedric, and Brian will counsel us.

[Dawn reads, as follows.]

> Janice, bursting into tears before she makes her opening remarks, charges that her husband has been having improper relationships with several (four) women in their church. Cedric (her husband) says that there are no real problems except with his wife's attitude. As the session develops, it becomes clear that the wife has confronted each of these women with her charges. The women variously became angered, tried to

explain that they were only friendly (they worked on the same committee), etc., but all four strongly denied any impropriety on their part or by Cedric. Cedric insists that there is no significant problem except his wife's imagination and jealousy. Counseling further disclosed that they had gone for six months to a Christian psychologist. There were no positive results. They both claim that he stated that their case was hopeless. Cedric and Janice agreed that they had reached the conclusion that they were as they were because that was they way God had made them. "And, after all," Cedric said, "married life is just one set of problems after another."

[Role play follows.]

Counselor: Here, Janice, have a Kleenex. [Janice mops her eyes.] Now, Cedric, what have you been up to, to give your wife such an impression? *Have* you been having "improper relationships" with women in your church? Tell me, what is it that you've been doing to bring Janice to this state? Have you been involved in adultery?"

Cedric: Absolutely not! You've got it all wrong, preacher. I haven't done anything. It's all in my wife's head! She's the one at fault, not me.

Counselor: Is that *really* how it is? Are you sure that you're not hiding something? If you are, remember, if you repent God will forgive you.

Cedric: How many times do I have to tell you? It's her imagination. That's all there is to it.

Counselor: Janice, are you sure about your accusations? Tell me what has happened.

Janice: I couldn't be more sure if I were standing beside him when he does it! I'm not blind – I know what he's like. There's no doubt about it. You should see him with those four women. They hang around him at church and he laughs and carries on with them – why it's disgraceful! I'm so embarrassed about it that I could…well, I'll leave it at that!

Counselor: And you confronted them. Well, what did they have to say for themselves?

Janice: They denied it to my face! What else would you expect of women who are caught? I'm not like many wives who would be afraid to confront them – you can be sure that I let them know what I thought about their behavior!

Counselor: That's reasonable enough. I guess that's what you'd expect from guilty people. Can you throw any more light on this matter, Cedric?

Cedric: Talk about embarrassed – how do you think I feel? I'm the laughingstock of the church! And, now, all four women avoid me like I had the plague.

Counselor: I guess you can understand that, can't you?

Cedric: Without a doubt. They don't like being falsely accused any more than I do!

Counselor: Are you sure you're not hiding something? It helps to come clean if you are.

Cedric: I've had it! I'm tired of being accused of something I didn't do. Don't expect to see me next week.

Counselor: I can understand why the psychologist gave up on you with an attitude like that. I suggest that you both go home and pray about the matter. I'm sure that God will bring a resolution in time if…

Greg: [Pleasantly, Greg says:] No, no. NO! Pious talk covering failure to come up with a biblical answer simply won't do! This is a typical "He said/she said" situation. You were stuck, but you didn't admit it to your counselees. Instead, you tried to cover up the fact with pious, insincere talk.

Brian: Ugh! You're right. I sure did flop, didn't I?

Greg: Yes, but that's OK. I didn't expect you to get it the first time. Here, let's change seats, Brian. Let me be the counselor. OK?

Brian: Great! I'm glad to get off this hot seat! [All laugh. The two switch seats.]

Greg: Now, let's be clear about matters, Janice. You've made a very serious charge against Cedric and four of your fellow church members. To do so, you must have some very convincing evidence – please tell me what it is.

Janice: If you were to see them hanging around one another at church, you'd know! A wife can tell these things.

Cedric: They're just friendly – that is they used to be! I can't help talking to them about matters that pertain to the committee that we're on together.

Janice: Huh! Laughing, having a good time! Do you call that talking?

Greg: Janice, I asked you for evidence that supports your charges. Surely you have more than your own subjective evaluation of what's been happening. Please tell me what it is.

Janice: I tell you, anyone can see what's going on if he has his eyes open. I don't need any more evidence than what I've seen myself. I just don't know how far it's gone. I do know that when they go to committee meetings, he picks up one of them!

Greg: So, you don't really have any *hard* evidence? Nothing objective? Only what *you* think is happening?

Janice: What do you mean by that?

Greg: I mean the testimony of eyewitnesses that Cedric has been acting "inappropriately." Or some physical evidence – like letters, or something of the sort.

Janice: Nothing like that. I don't go behind my husband's back asking others what they think of his behavior! But I know from personal observation – testimony enough – that he's got his eyes on them.

Cedric: See, she can't substantiate anything. I...

Greg: Just a minute, Cedric. I'm talking to Janice right now. You'll have a chance later. Janice, I want to read you a couple of verses. Jesus said, "If I testify about Myself, My testimony will not hold true," and He went on to say that He needed the testimony of others as well to make it valid (see John 5:31). That means, unless you have testimony outside of yourself, you don't have valid evidence. And Paul said in II Corinthians 13:1, "Every charge must be substantiated by the mouth of two or three witnesses." Paul wanted no accusations made to him when he went to Corinth unless they could be backed up with testimony.

Janice: Well, that was Corinth!

Greg: Yes, but that's also South Carolina, Alaska, and Nevada too! You claim to believe God's Word, don't you?

Janice: Yes, certainly! But you...

Greg: Where is there any room for "buts," Janice? If God required such testimony then, did He change His mind later on? There's no record of such a change. Indeed, according to II Corinthians 13:1, just the opposite is true.

Janice: I suppose not.

Greg: Well, then, the requirement applies to you. When you married Cedric, you promised to love Him, didn't you?

Janice: Of course. It was part of the wedding ceremony.

Greg: But you haven't been living up to that vow, have you?

Janice: How's that?

Greg: According to I Corinthians 13:7, love "believes all things, hopes all things." But you won't believe Cedric when he tells you that there's nothing to your charges. This verse also means that love gives the benefit of the doubt. You should hope (expect) the best and believe the best of him.

Janice: Even when my eyes tell me otherwise?

Greg: Even when your eyes tell you otherwise! Unless you have the kind of hard evidence that Jesus and Paul demanded, you must not make accusations about anyone – especially about your husband!

Janice: Well, I guess I can't exactly prove anything, but…

Greg: Again, why add the "but"? And the "exactly"? If you can't prove your claims, you must not make them. And not only must you stop, but you must begin to think the best – not the worst – of Cedric!

[End of Role Play]

Greg: I'm ending and stepping out of the role play to save time for discussion. As a counselor, I still have much to do, among which are:

1. Get a firm assent from Janice to cease and desist from making unfounded accusations, after repenting of those already made.

2. In a second session (perhaps) work on how she will go and seek forgiveness of the four women she has offended.

3. Strongly caution Cedric to cease doing anything that might even remotely occasion the slightest doubt on Janice's part, using I Corinthians 13 and I Peter 3:7 in doing so. Probe to obtain some concrete ways to establish greater trust.

4. Eventually, get into other problems in this troubled marriage. Possibly you will find that pre-marital sex occasioned suspicion, or previous incidents of various sorts, or whatever. Such may have led to mistrust, but not necessarily so.

5. Deal with their twisted attitudes toward God and toward marriage.

6. Work on communication.

7. In all, from beginning to end, give hope.

The order in which I have mentioned these seven items is not necessarily the one that would be followed in all cases, but would take its form from the drift of sessions. Flexibility must be shown here. OK. Now have at me – let's discuss my evaluation of the case.

Milt: Don't you think that you were too hard on Janice?

Greg: No, I don't. While the dialog that you've heard may be a bit briefer and more rapid than in the real counseling situation, I would say essentially the same things. Who was making the accusations?

Milt: Obviously, Janice.

Greg: Who was the immediate problem? Janice. Now, it's possible that further counseling may uncover other problems, doubtless some by Cedric. But we have only one before us at the moment. Don't try to do everything at once.

Bob: I think that Cedric had given up, soured on marriage, and was now blaming God. He needed a reprimand for his view of God, but also hope that somehow this matter could be resolved. Going after the main perpetrator of the immediate problem – Janice – I believe gave him hope for the first time in some time.

Greg: I think you are absolutely right. Cedric will get his "come-uppings" at a later time, and then Janice will get more hope too. He must be told that marriage need not be one set of problems after another, but that it can be one solution after another – and, in time, one joy after another. There is just so much that can be done at one time. So-called "he said/she said" impasses do not occur when two believers follow God's

Word. While the world has no answers to such situations, it's because they have nowhere to turn except to human wisdom.

Jane: What do you think Janice meant by "improper relationships?"

Greg: Something having to do with being too close to other women – perhaps hinting at sexual relations. But because she doesn't really know – and is only filled with suspicion – she's forced to use indefinite terms. That, in itself, is a clue to the fact that there was no real evidence.

Phil: How could the biblical counselor have given this couple hope at the outset, even after they had gone to a psychologist for six months with no positive results?

Greg: Good question. After so long, and with no success, you would expect that they were coming as a last resort – with, therefore, little hope. Possibly, if the counselor saw this as necessary at the outset, he could have said something like, "Hmmm. I see that you gave six months to your previous counselor. How about giving me six weeks?"

Phil: Would you have been able to help them in six weeks?

Greg: Yes. Not that everything would have been settled, but the basic problem they came with, plus a solid solution to it, should have been dealt within six weeks – or less. Other problems might have carried counseling on for a bit longer. This is a marriage that can sing if Cedric and Janice do what God requires. I can see communication, leading to a new relationship, blossoming. The meaning of love – beyond the first reference to it from I Corinthians 13 – will have to be discussed, and they will have to begin *giving*, she her trust toward him, he his attention toward her. Janice's repentance and confession to these four women will go a long way toward reconciliation all around. It's possible that to facilitate matters (and to make sure that no false step is taken that will only exacerbate matters) the counselor may go with her as she seeks them out.

The reference to the oath she took at the wedding ceremony was important, since God says that oaths must be kept – even to ones' own hurt! It would be important to stress (later) that when he took his marriage vows, Cedric also took an oath, not only to "love" but also to "honor" his wife. In several ways, he needs to see how this applies to himself. Both Janice and Cedric have some repenting to do.

Jane: Wow! I never knew there was so much to a case.

Bob: Exactly. And we've been here long enough. Let's save the next case for the next session together.

Phil: [teasing] Want extra time to get your case up to snuff – after our colossal failure to see how the biblical principals of solid testimony and love apply? [After some other light banter, there is prayer. All leave.]

CHAPTER EIGHTEEN

[Once more the group assembles as agreed upon. There is some stir among several members of the participants.]

Greg: Good to see you all again. Hope this has been a good week for you. I suppose you're all getting ready for finals and looking forward to the following semester. Busy days, I'm sure.

Milt: You can say that again! In fact, that's exactly what I want to tell you. Bob and I had determined to role play case #60, page 120, but we just couldn't find time to prepare it.

Bob: Right. With all the work they piled on us, here at the end, it's hard to find time to breathe! By all rights we probably shouldn't even be here today, but we knew you had set time apart for us, so here we are confessing our failure. And we had to tell you in person that we didn't prepare the case.

Greg: Well, I'm sorry you aren't prepared, but thanks for coming to tell me in person. But the world hasn't come to an end yet. I think that your present dilemma may afford an opportunity to stress some more nouthetic principles and practices.

Milt: I'm glad we didn't totally waste everyone's time.

Greg: Let me ask you, Bob and Milt, are you under the gun because of failure to keep up during the school year, or is this additional work that has been heaped on you?

Bob: Well...

Milt: Come on, Bob, you know as well as I how we tend to procrastinate. Sure. Much of our present dilemma is due to goofing off when we should have had our noses in the books. We left a lot of work to do to the end of the semester. Nouthetically speaking, there's no excuse for our problem,.

Bob: You're right Milt. We shouldn't be like so many others – cramming at the last minute. I'm sure that if we had been "following our responsibilities" (good nouthetic advice) throughout the semester we'd be a lot more relaxed at this point.

Greg: Well, I'm glad that you see it for yourselves. Living a structured life is a biblical requirement for Christians.

Bob: Don't tell me there's a nouthetic method for study!

Greg: Not really. The fact is, we're talking about a way of life that God wants the Christian to adopt in all areas.

Milt: Tell us about it.

Greg: In II Thessalonians 3:6–12, Paul chided those who were living in what he called "a totally unstructured way" (v. 11) for their idleness. He insisted that they get to work instead (v. 12). They were mooching off other Christians rather than earning their keep, but the principle is broader than the use of finances. It has to do with all of life, therefore, it has to do with study. It has to do with a pattern of life that grows out of responsible stewardship, of money, or, as in your case, of time. This pattern of structured living allows one to live in "quietness," as Paul noted in verse twelve. The hectic, unstructured life that accompanies irresponsible living is unbecoming to a believer. Instead, he ought to be cool, collected, and on top of things. Unstructured living causes difficulty for others as well as a great deal of worry, upset and consternation for one's self. Since you're all headed into a new semester, this is a perfect time to plan out how you ought to spend your time and energy to achieve the biblical way of life. Set up schedules and keep them. The last-minute study that many students saddle themselves with is unbiblical.

Bob: Good advice.

Milt: Sure, but about those schedules: to schedule everything seems so binding, so cramping…

Greg: Actually, a schedule is what frees you up to make changes. It is the route to flexibility!

Milt: How's that?

Bob: I can't see it either.

Greg: I'll try to explain. Let me take my own situation as an example. I used to think the same way about scheduling as you do. But before I began using a monthly planner my life was often chaotic. Often my best intentions were thwarted as plans were upset. When I finally realized that I was living irresponsibly, I began to use a planner to schedule things, and my life settled down.

Milt: I still don't get it.

Greg: It was something like this: writing out appointments in the planner I always knew if someone asked me to do something or other whether I had time for it or not. For the first time I was able to say "no" with a clear conscience. I could say, "Sorry, I see by my schedule that I already have that time committed." It was then easy to turn down a lot of unnecessary things, and things that I didn't want to do anyway. On the other hand, if something came up that I wanted to do, but was at the same time as I had scheduled something else, I could do some thoughtful decision-making. If I saw that it was possible to move the scheduled activity to another equally acceptable time, I could do so – because I knew where the empty spaces in my schedule were located. That gave me the maximum flexibility necessary to change events without guilt. Unless you schedule, you'll find that you don't have control of your time – others will take over your life! And, if you don't schedule commitments, you'll often be at a loss to know whether to say "yes" or "no" to an invitation – or, "well, how about this other time that I see I have free?" In order to assume your responsibilities, you need order! And order brings quietness into life rather than frustration. All we're talking about is good stewardship of time.

Phil: I guess you're right. If we don't plan our wedding carefully, for instance, Jane and I will be in trouble.

Jane: Don't worry about that! I'm already on top of the matter. I've just about drawn up all the necessary plans.

Phil: Whoof!

Greg: In counseling, you'll find that, in addition to other problems, many people have complicated their lives by drifting into irresponsible living patterns. You'll be teaching people how to structure their lives all the time. It is only through structure – regularity, commitment-keeping, consistency, etc. – that they can instill the new godly patterns that God wants them to put on. These new ways are adopted only by those who regularly do them – whether they feel like it or not. You've heard that before, but it's important to stress, since we live in a feeling-oriented society. You can hardly help others with this unless you first have learned to live that way yourselves.

Milt: OK. I think I've got it.

Bob: I'm heading for the campus bookstore as soon as I leave to buy a monthly planner!

Greg: Good. Now, what else do you want to discuss today? Or, rather than do so, would you like to exercise some flexibility and close our discussion now so you can get back to studying?

Phil: A great idea.

Greg: Since we seem to have run out of steam anyway, it would probably be a good idea, so, unless there's something else you simply must say, speak now, or forever after hold your peace...

Jane: [laughing at Greg's allusion to marriage] Does that mean we're through these discussions?

Greg: That's entirely up to you.

Phil: We'll *plan* to discuss it, and get back to you. [There is prayer, and the group leaves.]

CHAPTER NINETEEN

[Three weeks later, Greg receives an email that reads:]

Dear Pastor Greg,

Sorry we haven't gotten back to you before this, but with finals, papers, settling into a new location, well…I'm sure you understand. Since Brian and I have enrolled in Scriptural Presbyterian Seminary, we've lost touch with the rest of our group…except Jane, of course! And she's been out looking for a job. We'd like to meet with you tomorrow at 3PM if possible.

Thanks,
Phil

[Greg responds:]

Hi Phil!

Sure, let's meet. But make it at 3:30. I won't be able to get free till then. Looking forward to seeing you again.

Blessings,
Greg

[It's the next day. Precisely at 3:30 the threesome arrive at the church.]

Greg: Hi, gang. What's up?

Jane: Things have been happening so fast since I saw you that my head's spinning.

Greg: Tell me about them.

Brian: As Phil said in his email, we've all moved ahead with our plans. But Phil and I have a number of questions about S.P. Seminary…

Phil: And we all want to talk about joining your church.

Greg: Well, it looks as if we've got a lot of important matters to discuss. Who's first?

Brian: Can we begin with SPS?

Greg: Certainly. What's on your mind?

Brian: Just this – the seminary doesn't teach nouthetic counseling. In fact, they have a course called "Pastoral Counseling" that's taught by a psychologist. How could a psychologist teach pastoral anything?

Greg: Brian, I understand your problem. At this point, those of us who want to change that are still in the minority. But we're working on it.

Brian: Did we make a mistake in enrolling there?

Greg: That depends. What did you intend to get out of your seminary training? If you remember, I didn't say a word about learning counseling. I said that what you needed to learn is theology, the biblical languages and exegesis. In addition to those essentials, you'll have a fine Church History professor and an excellent Homiletic prof to boot. I didn't promise you training in nouthetic counseling.

Phil: Uh…Come to think of it, I guess you didn't.

Brian: So, you're saying that we'll have to get it on our own.

Greg: Precisely!

Phil: How do we go about doing that?

Greg: As I see it you have two options: either work through nouthetic counseling books, tapes and other helps, or take the two-year, 180 hour in-class Monday night course in nouthetic counseling offered at our church.

Jane: Now I remember you mentioning that class, but it dropped off my radar screen. Can I attend as well as the men?

Greg: The course is open to pastors, elders, seminary students, and key laymen. You'd all be more than welcome!

Brian: Great! I'll do it.

Phil: Me too.

Jane: Count me in.

Greg: Fine. The new course began last week, but you can still get in. It won't be difficult for you to catch up.

Phil: Can we get credit for this course and substitute it for the psych course?

Greg: I'm afraid not. Since they still haven't seen the light, the Seminary doesn't recognize our course – even though it is far more extensive. But there are five of our second year students at the seminary, and several who will enroll together with you for the first year.

Brian: Ah! So we won't have to fight the battles alone.

Greg: That's true, Brian. But though you will engage the professor from time to time, I hope you'll refrain from any sort of thing as that which happened at Christian U.

Brian: I've already thought about that. I'll work hard on controlling myself.

Phil: I'll be glad to meet with you each day we have that class to pray for help for us both.

Greg: Thanks, Phil. You see, though we're still in the minority, we're gaining support, and I'd not want anything to set back the progress we've already made.

Brian: Gotcha! I'll be good.

Jane: How did SPS get this way? It's a conservative school, isn't it?

Greg: Yes. But long before nouthetic counseling came to the fore, they instituted the practice of teaching psychology to help pastors meet the needs of their people. It was an unbiblical approach; they should have developed their own biblical counseling course. But they didn't. They meant well, but went astray. We discussed academia a few weeks ago, and how difficult it is to change anything once it's established. Well, the factors that we noted in academia in general are in place at SPS as well.

Phil: I see. At least you offer an alternative. And when Brian and I are ordained, that will be two more voices to hear from.

Greg: Good. But be wise as serpents and harmless as doves, as Jesus said.

Jane: Now, can we talk about joining your church?

Greg: Certainly. In your case, Jane, we decided to wait until after your marriage so that you could get pre-marital counseling from your pastor and be married in your current church.

Jane: That's what we decided. But you also mentioned the matter of doctrinal agreement before marriage. I have been working hard to understand infant baptism and I admit I'm having a hard time. The one scenario that Brian presented to me has me stumped at the moment, however.

Greg: What was that?

Jane: Why don't you tell him Brian?

Brian: OK. Here it is. It's the day before Pentecost. Andrew, a pious Jewish father, has just had his child circumcised. He is happy because he now knows that little Simeon is a part of the covenant community – the visible church. The next day, he hears Peter preach and believes the Gospel. Now, according to Baptist thought, his child is no longer in the visible church. In for one day and out the next. She hasn't been able to get around that one!

Jane: Yeah, but there must be some answer to it. I just haven't had time to figure it out biblically.

Phil: I haven't been pushing Jane to say that she believes something when she doesn't. That's no way to help anyone come to truth. Or to establish a marriage.

Greg: How right you are, Phil. I won't do so either. But at any time you want to discuss the matter, I'll be available. Now, what about church membership?

Brian: Phil and I want to become members as soon as possible. I suppose that we'll have to take a membership course or something first, right?

Greg: Wrong. Some churches require such membership courses, but we don't think that is biblical. The Bible shows that once a person understood the Gospel and believed, he was admitted into membership. We think we should do the same. In the great commission the apostles were told to "teach" converts "to observe" what Christ commanded *after* they were baptized. That's exactly what we do. We consider becoming a member on a par with matriculating into a school. You have joined to learn. Calvin called the church "Christ's school." So, once you've entered this "school" it's our job to teach you all that we can. You don't stop learning once you "graduate" from some membership class (never to study again!).

Jane: Well, I'm going to keep working on it.

Phil: And Brian and I will help her.

Greg: Now, what else can I do for you today?

Phil: I have a question about seminary. Jane and I will be married some day soon, I trust, even though the baptism matter is temporarily holding things up. I am going to try to get a part-time job too since I want to contribute something to my family. I don't want Jane to have to do it all. But will that adversely effect my studies? Should I stretch out my program for an extra year or two? I'd hate to do so, since I can hardly wait to get into the ministry.

Jane: I tell him that it's OK with me that he doesn't work. I'll support us for three years. Why extend it to four? That only makes it more difficult for the both of us. What do you think?

Greg: I can't decide this one for you since only Phil can know his capacity. Can he hold a job and study effectively as well?

Phil: I don't know. But I do know that I am going to earn at least a part – however small – of our keep!

Greg: Well, if you're insistent, then let me utter some academic heresy that you can take or leave! Since you are not considering going for a doctorate in order to teach – right Phil?...

Phil: Definitely! I want to be on the front lines.

Greg: All right. Since you aren't, then consider this. Is it necessary to work for all As?

Phil: You mean grades?

Greg: Exactly. Does the Bible – or only academia – require high grades?

Brian: That's easy – only academia.

Greg: Then, if Brian's right, why not aim for Bs or even some Cs, and spend the rest of the time and energy that this frees up in caring for your family? Of course, you must really do so, if you take this (generally thought) "ill-advised" suggestion. There can be no goofing off in front of TV or in any other manner. Don't decide now. Get your part-time job, try things out and see if you need to scale back on your studies. You ought to know almost as much psychology as the prof does by now, so perhaps that's the first place to slack off. Whatever you decide to do, get your theology and your languages down pat. Now, I suggest this option with fear and trembling because I know that it could be abused.

Phil: Wow! You certainly are unorthodox – that is, in every way except biblically!

Greg: I'll take that as a compliment. Brian, all you must do to unite with our church, since you've been baptized is have your church send a letter of good standing to ours. And Phil, since, your church isn't a Bible-believing Presbyterian church, we'll have to examine you for a profession of faith. In all cases, we have new members appear before the elders and give their assent to the membership questions. Then, they repeat their answers before the congregation which formally welcomes them into membership. These questions have to do with your salvation, your desire to live for Christ and your willingness to submit to the authority of Christ invested in the eldership of our church according to Hebrews 13:17. Here is a copy of the questions for each of you. Take them with you and be sure you can answer them in the affirmative before we set a date. If there is anything you don't understand, I'll be glad to help you do so.

Brian: I believe we've heard enough today to send us off with some new thoughts.

Jane: I agree.

Phil: Me too.

[Pastor Greg prays and all leave.]

CHAPTER TWENTY

[Phil and Brian join Greg's church. Jane greets them after the morning service.]

Jane: Well, you did it!

Brian: I certainly did, and am I glad! Two Mondays ago when we all began the First Principles of Biblical Counseling class my heart was so stirred I could hardly stand it. Just think – to actually attend a counseling session in which Scripture, and the God Who gave it, is exalted above man's wisdom. What a contrast to the psychology class at Christian U! And there it was all the time in II Timothy 3:15–17, and elsewhere in Scripture, just waiting for someone to show us the sufficiency of the Scriptures. This is going to be a great Monday evening course.

Jane: I agree. And I couldn't put it more forcefully.

Phil: Nor could I. And now, Brian, we're a part of the congregation too. The message this morning was a great blessing as Pastor Greg opened up the Scriptures and not only showed us what they mean, but how their truth can be implemented in our lives. It looks like nouthetic counseling and biblical preaching complement one another.

Jane: Right. After greeting us, most of the members of the congregation have gone home. Perhaps we could corner Greg for a couple of minutes to thank him for all he's done for us.

Brian: Great idea. There he is – greeting the last person to leave.

Phil: Greg! We want to thank you so much for all the time, patience, instruction and guidance you've given to us. You surely went beyond the call of duty.

Jane & Brian: Amen!

Greg: I'm just happy God used it in your lives. And we're delighted to have you as a part of our congregation.

Jane: I'm not a member yet, and we've not announced a wedding date since I'm still struggling with the infant baptism issue. But I hope soon to get that matter settled. Then, if all goes well, after the wedding, I want to join too.

Greg: You want to be sure of your convictions. Be certain that Phil isn't the motive! Have you found an answer to Brian's conundrum?

Jane: No. And it bothers me. I've read Adams' book, *The Meaning and Mode of Baptism,* and that took care of the mode matter. But I'm still at sea about paedobaptism. And any decision I make will be with unmixed motives.

Greg: Hang in there and keep studying. Remember, I'm available to discuss the question, should you desire to do so.

Jane: I know that, but right now I think I want to put together the pieces of the puzzle for myself, if I can. I am sure the Bible has the answer, and I hope to find it.

Greg: Be assured – it does!

Phil: Well, I guess we'll be going now.

Brian: Thank God our plans for the future have been crystallized in a Scriptural way.

Greg: Yes. But, of course, you have yet to graduate from S.P. Seminary, be called to a congregation and undergo examination and ordination by the Presbytery. Things could change along the way, but if God wants both of you in some ministry that's where you will be! He'll clear the path ahead for you. That doesn't mean that the way will necessarily be easy, but it will be certain.

Jane: We'll see you tomorrow night.

Greg: Goodbye, and the Lord bless you.

[All exit and go their ways.]

AFTERWORD

By Greg Dawson

As I write these words, eight months have passed since Phil and Brian united with First Scriptural Presbyterian Church. Phil Beckham is now married to the former Jane Millhouse who, after struggling with baptism, came to a firm position. My problem now is to keep her from accosting every Baptist she meets about the subject! Jane has a good job in a bank where she has advanced quickly to a position where she now trains new employees. Phil is going to seminary, and the state pays him to read law books onto CDs for a blind law student. He has not yet received a grade lower than a B. Brian Donlevy remains unmarried, with no prospects in view. He is an outstanding student at the Seminary, and is turning out to be an effective preacher. His parents support him. As for Milt, Dawn, and Bob, there is little to report. Milt is completing his psychology studies at Christian U, and plans to do counseling in a Christian school. Dawn married an engineer and moved to Grand Rapids. Bob has changed his major twice and remains unsettled about his future.

By Philip Beckham

Pastor Greg graciously allowed me the opportunity to address a few words to the readers of this book. I want to encourage any of you who might have doubts about nouthetic counseling to consider the matter very carefully. I have learned much from interviewing Greg, but a lot more from the Monday night course. As a matter of fact, I have found it possible to begin counseling several of my fellow students at SPS. And it seems that Jane is always helping someone or other. I encourage you to get training in nouthetic counseling for yourself. Nouthetic counseling books, together with study of the distance learning course offered by the Institute for Nouthetic Studies, probably provide the very best opportunity for training that is now available. The

Institute course involves lectures by Adams and others. Oh, one more thought – don't believe the gossip about nouthetic counseling. I can testify, in the face of all contrary claims, that such gossip is false, and that nouthetic counseling is truly biblical. May God use this record of our interviews to help you as well as many others.

Appendix A

What Makes Nouthetic Counseling Unique?

Introduction

I am using the word unique in its true sense – to describe something that is above all else incapable of degrees. Nouthetic counseling is unique – it is one-of-a-kind!

NOUTHETIC COUNSELING IS UNIQUE...

I. Because the Atmosphere of Your Sessions is Unique

    A. You counsel in a unique environment.
        1. You don't counsel alone; you team counsel.
        2. "How's that unique?" you ask.
        3. Just this way – the Holy Spirit is the other counselor in the room.
        4. You don't counsel in your own wisdom and power alone.

    B. You will let your counselee know this fact.
        1. You will make it clear that in counseling he must deal with God.
        2. All decisions/promises, etc., are made to God, ultimately: not to the counselor.
        3. What you do will impress this fact upon him.
            a. You will pray.
            b. You will use Scripture authoritatively.
            c. You will use biblical language and labels.
            d. You will, yourself, submit to God in all you do and say.

II. Because Those You Counsel Are Unique

    A. They are transformed people, "saints" (people "set apart" by God).
        1. Down deep, they have the right desires (Romans 7:15, 19).

2. They are capable of change that pleases God.
   a. Which is not true of others (Romans 8:8).
   b. That's why we counsel Christians alone [explain fully].
3. Our counselees don't always act as they should.
   a. But they *are capable* of doing so.
   b. Counseling is done to help them please God.

B. The Holy Spirit dwells in them...
   1. To give right desires and power to change and obey God (Philippians 2:13; Ephesians 1:19–20).
   2. He helps them pray (Romans 8:26,27);
   3. And helps them fight sin (Galatians 5:17) in order to produce good fruit (Galatians 5:18).
   4. He makes them capable of understanding and appropriating Scripture (I Corinthians 2).

III. Because Your Objectives Are Unique

A. The Goal of others: help counselees...
   1. By reaching solutions to their problems in order to...
   2. Bring relief.

B. Often an unattainable goal
   1. Relief may never come.
   2. E.g., a wife may get the divorce anyway.

C. Their objective is wrong...
   1. Because it is man-centered...
   2. And omits God.

D. Your ultimate objective will be to help the counselee to please God in his situation...
   1. Whether or not relief is forthcoming.
   2. This objective can always be reached, no matter what happens, when you counsel Christians...
   3. If out of love they will obey God.

E. Even your proximate goal (or objective} is unique.

1. It is to honor God by breaking the sanctification log-jam in your counselee's life...
2. So he can continue to become more like Christ (note Colossians 1:28).

IV. Because Your Methods Are Unique

A. Everyone listens and talks in counseling (these are means and are not unique).

B. But methods are means committed to the ends of a system.
1. Since your prime objective is to honor God, your methods must do so.
2. Yours, therefore, will grow out of and be consistent with Scripture at every point.

C. So, you will not import methods from other systems...
1. In which the analysis of problems is wrong.
2. And it also would be foolish to do so since their objectives are different.
3. And their methods are designed to attain those wrong ends.
4. Yours must be designed to meet the goals God set in the Bible.

D. Examples of unique Christian methods
1. Prayer
2. Repentance, leading to fruit (Luke 3:8ff.)
3. Church discipline
   a. A right and a blessing to every believer
   b. Through which Christ promises to help (Matthew 18:19)

V. Because Your Setting Is Unique

A. You counsel under the aegis of the church, meshing with its ministry.
1. Churches don't have counseling centers.
2. By definition, they are such – even when they neglect the work.

B. Cf. Acts 20:31; I Thessalonians 5:12, 13.

C. [Read quote from Calvin's commentary on Acts 20:20, 31.]

D. You have all of the resources of Christ's church to call upon

VI. Because Your Incentives Are Unique

A. What happens in counseling has eternal consequences for all involved.
   1. Colossians 3:23, 24 speaks of an "inheritance" that is involved.
   2. "Heavenly treasures" are at stake (Matthew 6:19, 20).

B. And you know that God's promises don't fail.
   1. Cf. II Peter 1:3; I Corinthians 10:13.
   2. All the resources needed for life and godly living are in the Bible (see also II Timothy 3:15–17).
   3. And there is the Spirit to spur you on (Philippians 2:13).

VII. Because Your Results Are Unique

A. When you help Christians, God is pleased, glorified (Matthew 15:16).

B. Counselees are edified (II Corinthians 13:10).

C. And, even when all seems to fail, if the Word was faithfully ministered, it will achieve God's purposes (Isaiah 55:10, 11).

Conclusion

These factors are unique because *Jesus is unique.*

The word *monogenes,* mistranslated "only-begotten (John 3:16, etc.), really ought to be translated *"unique"* The Greek word means "The only one of its kind." A wise Christian counselor takes advantage of his unique resources, while trusting in God's unique son!

Appendix B

What to Expect
from
Christian Counseling

By Jay E. Adams

Help for Those Considering Counseling

1
Behind Closed Doors

Congratulations! You've been thinking of receiving Christian counseling. There's nothing better that you could do when it's necessary for you to get help. Indeed, if you are still hesitating, I hope that this little booklet will help you to decide to make the move.

If there's some hesitation on your part, perhaps it's because you don't know what counseling would involve. After all, counseling is always done behind closed doors – as, of course, it should be. Let me open those doors a crack and give you some idea of what might take place.

Obviously, not every counseling problem is the same, nor is every counselee or counselor exactly alike. So you may expect some variation from what you read here, though you should find the basics the same.

In solving problems, Christian counselors are committed to helping their counselees change in ways that please God. In order to do so, they prayerfully discuss these problems in the light of the Bible. They help counselees discover what God's Word teaches and how it applies to daily living. They are interested not only in *what* must be done to please God, but also in *how* to go about achieving it. To do this, they help counselees frame specific ways of implementing biblical commands and monitor their progress in obeying them. And in doing these things, they are vitally concerned about a counselee's relationship to Christ and His church.

Take time to peruse the rest of this booklet, where particular aspects of the counseling process are set forth. If there is something that you don't understand, that is not covered here or that causes you some concern, be sure to inquire about it from your potential counselor.

2
The Atmosphere of Counseling

You are going to find a Christian atmosphere in truly biblical counseling. That means several things. First, the Standard for all that is said and done will be the Scriptures of the Old and New Testaments. That means that at all times your counselor will seek to say and do nothing more or less than what the Bible teaches. If at any point you are doubtful about the way things are proceeding, your counselor will be happy to explain why – biblically – counseling is progressing as it is. Simply ask. Some things that you must do will involve direct biblical commands while others will be done by implication. But there will always be a Scriptural reason for whatever is done.

Secondly, you can expect your counselor to pray. He may pray before, during or after the session. But, since he believes that the Holy Spirit, using His Word, is the One Who changes people, he will certainly ask Him for such help.

Next, counseling will stress the fact that the prime relationship in each session is not that which exists between the counselor and the counselee. Rather; it is always the relationship between the counselee and God that is uppermost. The counselor is but the facilitator, who ministers the Word which brings God and the counselee together in a vital relationship. Counselees will be encouraged, therefore, to obey God – not the counselor. Failure to heed God's Word is not merely a matter of failing to hear the counselor; it is disobedience to God.

Because God has provided answers for all of "life and god-liness" (II Peter 1:3) there is no valid counseling problem that He cannot solve. That, however, does not mean that your counselor knows all the answers. He will expect you to pray for him, therefore, that God will enable him to discover and deploy just the right biblical answers to your situation.

As a result of the biblical orientation of Christian counseling, you can expect your) counselor to give you down-to-earth, clear, explanations in biblical language. Your counselor will not speak in jargon – psychological or otherwise. Problems and their solutions will be discussed from the point of view of what God has to say about them in the Bible.

God's power to change lives in ways that please Him, is available only to believers. If you are not a Christian – one who has been saved by grace through faith in Jesus Christ – then you need first of all to speak: to your potential counselor about this matter. If this is all confusing he will be glad to explain the gospel to you. Since God's solutions to problems are available only to His children, no matter what outward changes you may make you "cannot please God" until you trust in Jesus Christ (Romans 8:8). That is why your counselor will want to precounsel before attempting to counsel you.

3
Prepare for Counseling

You can speed up counseling by doing certain things.

First, before coming to counseling, you may gather all the data you can pertaining to your problem. Write out various questions you want answered, facts that may be of help and other information you think may be useful. Don't bring pages and pages of materials, however. Keep this written information brief, to the point and non-repetitious. It is probably best to limit it to statements rather than paragraphs. If you can, organize these according to topics.

When in counseling, explain everything that may be useful for helping your counselor to understand the situation. Answer his questions as fully as possible. Do not hold back facts: He cannot counsel properly apart from all the necessary data. What happens in counseling will largely consist of discussion and action taken upon the basis of these facts.

Moreover, do homework assignments fully and promptly. Lagging behind in this matter may greatly hinder progress. The principal work to be done is not that which the counselor and you do in counseling sessions but what you do in-between, during the week, at home and at work or school. It is there, in actual life situations, that you and God will work out the biblical principles and practices discussed and agreed upon in counseling sessions. The counseling session is not a magical hour in which the counselor "does it to you." Rather, during the session you and he decide from the Scriptures what God would have you do. Then, during the week following, by God's wisdom and strength you must go out into the milieu and do it.

It is important not to view your counselor in an adversarial position. It is true that he may often challenge you, point out sin in your life and advise you to do things that you do not want to do. The two of you may struggle together over some of these matters. But he will do these things because he wants to help and because, to be faithful to God and His Word, he must do so. He will want to maintain a coaching relationship rather and an adversarial one.

4

Know Your Problem

One *of* the first discussions that you and your counselor are likely to have may be about your agenda. He win want to ask, as Jesus did, "What do you want me to do for you?" (Mark 10:51, CCNT). It is important for him to know what your object is in seeking counsel. He will want you to be very clear about this. If you cannot state it precisely, say so. He will help you shape up your agenda according to biblical parameters. Even if you do have a clear objective in mind it is altogether possible that your counselor may wish to negotiate your agenda with you. Why? Because he will want to be sure

146

that the two *of* you are seeking to reach the same goals. Of even greater importance, he will be concerned that the goals stated are the same as those that God's Word sets forth. In negotiating your agenda, you counselor may focus on *prioritizing* your goals. If, for instance, you come seeking "relief" from some problem, he may point out that though that may be a valid goal, it cannot be the top one. Above all else, he will observe, you should seek to please God by doing His will in the matter – *whether or not the relief is obtainable.*

Your counselor may also wish to help you *classify* your problems. He may point out that some are principal problems (the most serious ones) and that others are complication problems. He may not always begin with principal problems, but may need to deal with complicating problems before he can do so. Complicating problems are often those which we create when we attempt unsuccessfully to solve problems. They come from failing to do what God wants us to do about them. This failure may stem from ignorance, from poor teaching and advice, from pride, leading to unwillingness to seek help sooner, or (more seriously) from rebellion.

Regardless of what else is done, you and your counselor will have to agree upon God's agenda for you or everything else that you do will be flawed. This, then, is an essential matter.

5

There is Hope for You

Typical of true Christian counseling sessions is the abundance of hope expressed by the counselor and offered to the counselee. This is true even when the problems considered may be of the gravest sort. How can that be?

Well, Christian counselors have good reasons to be hopeful. They know, far instance, that a genuinely regenerate person possesses all of the requisite resources to solve every legitimate counseling problem in a way that is pleasing to. Gad. Indeed, they see no possibility of failure so long as all concerned understand, accept and fallow the teachings of the

Scriptures. They have God's guarantees for success! They know, also, that not only is the Bible sufficient for solving problems, but that the Spirit, Whose power can bring about all needed changes in one's life, dwells within every believer, helping him to understand and implement its truth. What else is needed?

Other counseling systems have no such sufficient standard for living life and no such mighty power for helping counselees change and grow. Why, then, shouldn't the biblical counselor exude hope? Do not discount the hope that your counselor offers. According to 1 Thessalonians 1:3, hope, – which in the Bible means expectation of something that God says is certain to happen is necessary for – perseverance. Since in the process of dealing with your problems, you will probably need to do some difficult things, you will probably need hope to motivate you to do them.

Once more, let's be clear about where that hope comes from. Here is what God says:

> What was written before was written for our instruction, that by the endurance and the encouragement that the Scriptures give us we may have hope. Romans 15:3

Clearly, then, the solution to your problems will flow from the Bible That is why you will want to listen carefully to the passages of the Bible to which your counselor refers and to follow them explicitly. There is hope. And that hope lies in God. Paul wrote:

> Now may the God of hope give you every sort of joy and peace: in believing so that you may have an abundance of hope by the power of His Holy Spirit. Romans 15:13

6
Make the Most of Counseling

While we haven't covered much ground in this booklet, perhaps through it you have gleaned some idea of what counseling will be like. Much more will take place during the six to twelve weeks that you will be in counseling of course. But during that time you will have a good opportunity to examine your life as a Christian. Take advantage of this. Don't think only about the problem or problems that made you consider counseling in the first place. Rather take the opportunity to recommit yourself to the Lord Jesus Christ and to the work of His church. Straightening out problems ought to be but the prelude to greater growth in your spiritual life. Counseling is but a blip on the radar screen; you must see it simply as a way of turning obstacles into – challenges to become more like Christ. Having removed whatever obstacles inhibit growth you may go on to greater things for Him.

If this booklet has stimulated questions that it has not answered please feel free to ask your counselor about them. Most Christian counselors are delighted to receive thoughtful inquiries.

Finally, thank God that He has called the officers of the church to counsel formally, and others in the church to do so informally (I Thessalonians 5:12,13; Galatians 6:1,2). Ask Him to help you make the right decisions about counseling as you enter into. this important phase of Christian growth.